ATOMIC RANCH

MIDCENTURY INTERIORS

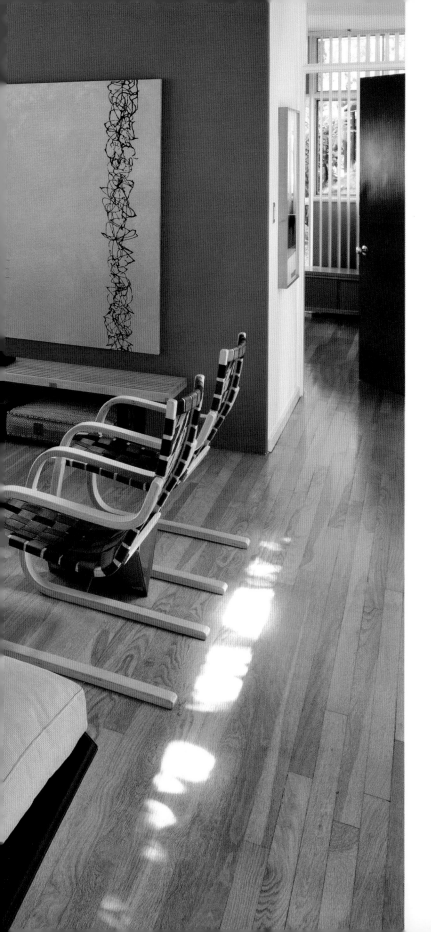

ATOMIC RANCH

MIDCENTURY INTERIORS

MICHELLE GRINGERI-BROWN
PHOTOGRAPHS BY JIM BROWN

GIBBS SMITH
TO ENRICH AND INSPIRE HUMANKIND

First Edition
16 15 14 13 12   5 4 3 2 1

Published by
Gibbs Smith
P.O. Box 667
Layton, Utah 84041

1.800.835.4993 orders
www.gibbs-smith.com

Designed by Debra McQuiston
Printed and bound in China

Gibbs Smith books are printed on either recycled, 100% post-consumer waste, FSC-certified papers or on paper produced from sustainable PEFC-certified forest/controlled wood source. Learn more at www.pefc.org.

Library of Congress Cataloging-in-Publication Data

Gringeri-Brown, Michelle.
  Atomic ranch midcentury interiors / Michelle Gringeri-Brown ; with photographs by Jim Brown. — 1st ed.
      p. cm.
  ISBN 978-1-4236-1931-4
1. Interior decoration—United States—History—20th century. 2. Ranch houses—United States. I. Brown, Jim (James Scott), 1951- II. Atomic ranch. III. Title.
  NK2004.G755 2012
  747.0973'09045—dc23
                    2011038361

We'd like to acknowledge the homeowners who generously opened their doors to us and spent countless hours fielding picky questions and sharing their love for their homes and midcentury design. To the enthusiasts in Cincinnati, Tulsa, and Washington, D.C., who came out for post-shoot dinners—it was great to meet you, and thanks for your proselytizing. To our editorial assistant, Cheyenne Tackitt, kudos for not screaming when we took on a second book. And a big thanks to our freelance graphic design team, who helped with the herculean job of preparing the images: Nancy Anderson, Carol Flores, and Dale Headrick. Last, but certainly not least, it was a pleasure to work with our Gibbs Smith editor, Bob Cooper, who sweats the details.

For those ardent Ranchers who've been eagerly anticipating this volume, hope it's all that you expected and more.

contents

FOREWORD

THERE IS A GOOD REASON the advertising images of the 1950s and '60s look so giddily happy: given the nation's then-recent history of economic privation and war, who wouldn't be overjoyed with sparkling clean dishes or a car that looked as good as the '55 Bel Air? The homes of that era similarly reflected the optimism and faith in the future that pervaded the times.

Our history is familiar but bears repeating: The Great Depression saw a peak nationwide unemployment of 25 percent and was exacerbated by the Dust Bowl in the Great Plains. World War II brought economic recovery but exacted a terrible human price. Seeking remedies for its citizens, the federal government instituted creative and wide-ranging programs to encourage higher education and home ownership, and established national residential construction standards. With these solid foundations, the returning GIs and the millions who awaited them at home helped fuel the housing boom of the midcentury period. And that provides the context for the eight homes we feature here.

Our 2006 book for Gibbs Smith, *Atomic Ranch: Design Ideas for Stylish Ranch Homes,* introduced the wide variety of postwar ranches and the historical roots of the style. And while our quarterly magazine explores these homes in more depth, we found that we wanted to dig even deeper into some exceptional examples, focusing on what makes their interiors so compelling while giving you ideas to apply to your own home.

Ranches are ubiquitous from coast to coast; wherever there was a housing boom, entrepreneurial builders included the style in their development mix. Two of our earliest homes (1954 and 1955), illustrate the stylistic range of the era: one is a brick and glass flat-roofed box, while the other is a traditional filled with time-capsule furnishings. Whether an open-floor-plan California modern, a split-level, or a basic rambler, ranches were by and large well-built, solid homes.

Traveling from New York to California, we found stylish tract homes (not an oxymoron), custom architectural designs, and anonymous builder houses with intriguing interiors. Each was chosen to celebrate the owners' solutions to living today in homes built half a century ago. While we focused on larger residences to make sure there were plenty of ideas to share, wonderful ranches can range from under 1,000 square feet to more than 4,000. Whatever the size, it is still a modest home style.

You'll note that interior design is highly personal. We've tried to give historical context to help you make informed decisions and avoid fleeting trends, but you'll see that some owners' choices differ from our advice or fly in the face of another's experience. The residents in this volume are all living contemporary lives, but they understand and acknowledge how they and their homes are grounded in the recent past. With luck and care, a house can last for a hundred years or more; these midcentury marvels will continue to influence us for a long time to come.

Jim Brown

DAYLIGHT RANCH, 1969

Portland, Oregon
4,130 square feet
4 bedrooms, 3.5 baths

WORK
OF ART

Located in a neighborhood the owner likens to a little Italian hill town, this West Hills home is incredibly close to the street yet still private.

◀ **OVERLEAF:** The entry hall is where the home's repetition of materials and design motifs is revealed: raw steel is used for the stair railing, display table, and doorframe, as well as around the new landscape window in the living room, seen beyond the divider screen. A painting by Christian Carlson hangs over the table, and overhead, a George Nelson bubble lamp nicely contrasts with the rectilinear elements of the room.

▶ **ALL THE WOOD** in the living room is new to the house, as are most of the furnishings. Though Mark loves the look of wood ceilings, they decided to leave the ceilings as they were and instead put the richness in the walls. The leather Albert sectional is from Design Within Reach and the chair is an Eames LCW (lounge chair, wood). The rug is an Odegard Oushak and the fierce-looking sculpture is an antique Japanese roof ridge cap.

A

ARCHITECTS HAVE A REPUTATION FOR LIVING IN MODERN GLASS BOXES with severe furniture and stark abstract art. But some, Mark Engberg for one, also have a soft spot for midcentury ranch houses.

The late-'60s home he now shares with his wife, Laurie, had been on the market for nearly a year when they first looked at it, so the listing Realtor just about broke a speed record getting there to show them around one Saturday. "When you date or are married to an architect, what you do on weekends is drive around and look at houses," Laurie says. "Mark had always wanted a midcentury house."

She was a little stunned by its lilac and pickled-oak interior, but Mark saw right past that to the modern architecture, the high ceilings, and east-facing walls of glass. The layout was typical for a Northwest hillside ranch, with the bedrooms on the daylight-basement level, while the living room, dining room, kitchen, mudroom, and powder room were upstairs. Inside the garage, Laurie noticed a beautiful exposed beam and the best views of Mount St. Helens and Mount Adams—a prophetic vision as it turned out.

The couple sold her home and his condo, bought the ranch, got married, and began refining the house, from the front facade to the garage and back again. "I've always trusted Mark's judgment; I knew that he has vision and that he would make sure it was a lovely home," says Laurie, 53, a college English instructor.

As the founding principal of COLAB Architecture + Urban Design in Portland, Oregon, Mark, 50, has more design skills and resources at his fingertips than most homeowners, yet the arc of the couple's remodel was still episodic and solution-based. Between them, the couple had a huge library, so their first project was bookshelves lining one long wall of the living room. Cherry paneling and new oak floors in the living and dining rooms followed, as did a steel-framed window overlooking the driveway.

"We wanted more light in that part of the living room—especially afternoon light—and because of the slope of the hill outside, all you can see is the earth,

no sky," Mark explains about what he terms their "landscape" window. "This was the first application of steel in the house, but I knew I was going to use it on the fireplace as well. I wanted to have materials other than wood and gypsum board; to me, steel is a material that is both rustic and slick—it is as smooth as glass."

A long but somewhat narrow space with a wall of windows on one end, the living room had some inherent challenges. A two-sided masonry fireplace divides the dining and living functions, and doorways to the entry hall and a deck further eat up wall space. This led to a major question any family can relate to: where to put the TV.

"The orientation of the fireplace to the side is the one design flaw of the house," Mark remarks. "It's not an easy room to place furniture in. We tried a separate seating area near the window, but no one ever used that."

To avoid craning their necks to the side to view a television on the one unbroken wall, the Engbergs stashed their set inside the firebox while Mark puzzled out a solution. He finally came up with the idea of partially wrapping the masonry fireplace surround with cherry panels and a patinated steel box that camouflages the flat-screen TV. A door slides up for viewing, and a simple steel shelf under the cantilevered hearth holds media peripherals.

"Because of the material, it looks kind of like a big metal hood in a ski lodge; I knew it would be OK with the heat," he explains.

Custom midcentury homes in the Northwest tend to use wood liberally—it is a region known for its timber, after all. An open plan with soaring ceilings in the public

◀ **HOUSING THE ENTERTAINMENT CENTER** on the fireplace involved building a steel box for the flat-screen television with a door that slides closed when not in use, and constructing a media tray under the floating hearth.

▼ **THIS REVERSE VIEW** shows the furniture placement obstacles, as well as the repetition of color in the dining room and entry hall, and the indoor/outdoor feel of the home— despite its two-level construction on a sloped lot. The cherry paneling, installed by Ron Downey of NWR Construction, was a challenge. "I was surprised that, although there were no signs of settlement, the house is not that square," says Mark Engberg. "It becomes a big deal when you're putting up paneling." Furnishings include a Tolomeo floor lamp, an Eames lounge chair and ottoman, a Quad coffee table, and West Elm accent lamps and tables.

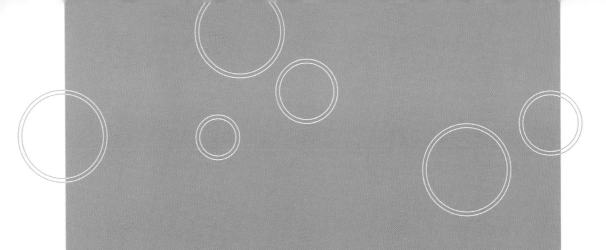

INTERIOR COLORS

THE POPULARITY OF CRAFTSMAN BUN-GALOWS has spawned a nationwide love affair with intense interior hues set off by white or natural wood molding. Cranberry-colored dining rooms and muddy taupe living rooms can be found from coast to coast. But midcentury ranch homes need a different approach.

Materials like brick, concrete block, mahogany paneling, and grass cloth were common original elements and, combined with large windows or walls of glass, establish a neutral palette. The open floor plan found in many ranches argues for continuity of color: if you're looking around your room wondering where the kitchen color should stop and the dining room color begin, odds are they should both be the same hue.

The palette you choose will be based on personal taste, the style of your house (traditional, modernist, or something in between), and often the region you live in. The bright pastels of Palm Springs and Miami might look garish in Denver or Indianapolis, with their different qualities of light and social conventions. And don't expect that your partner or spouse will necessarily agree on the "perfect" color you've chosen.

"I'm completely comfortable with lighter colors for interiors. I can appreciate a stark, gallery-white room,"
says Portland, Oregon, architect Mark Engberg. "I want the light to come in and for the room to be bright."

His wife, Laurie, however, came from an Arts and Crafts Foursquare to their 1969 ranch and lobbied for warmer colors in the dining room and foyer. They both agreed on a subdued green for those two rooms, and Mark thought he'd won the first round on the choice for the living room—bright white. But at the paint store, the color got creamier and less pristine.

"What we ended up with was kind of halfway down the middle, which is usually a bad idea. It's not what I wanted and it wasn't really what Laurie wanted," he says. "Later on we repainted it lighter, then ended up paneling it, which made both of us happy."

An online search for "midcentury paint colors" will give you links to scans from vintage paint catalogs, examples of original color schemes from builder Joseph Eichler, and blogs chronicling homeowners' experiences grappling with this topic. Period fabrics, wallpapers, and magazines are other sources for authentic midcentury colors, and most paint stores can color match any sample you bring in. While historic paint lines tend to focus on earlier architectural styles, California Paints includes "20th Century Eclecticism" in its collection and Sherwin-Williams has an inspiring "Suburban Modern" palette of interior and exterior shades.

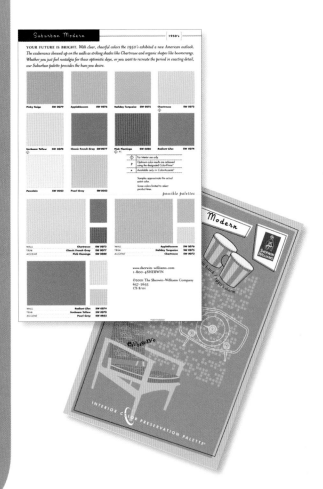

The layout is typical for a Northwest hillside ranch, with the bedrooms on the daylight-basement level.

Detached Garage

Deck

Master Suite

Stone Pavers

Bath

Turntable

Dining

Laundry

Kitchen

Powder Room

Deck

Walkway

Driveway

Dining Room

Fireplace

Living Room

rooms, lots of rich paneling, and small, stateroom-like bedrooms downstairs overlooking a sloping ravine is a recurring design theme. Although the Engbergs' beautiful finishes and fittings are of more recent vintage, their remodel makes use of these vernacular details. Nowhere is that more apparent than in the new kitchen and master bedroom.

The original kitchen had a U-shaped workspace with a breakfast nook beyond. Visually separated by upper cabinets, neither space worked particularly well and, with burnt orange walls, a red sink, white laminate cabinets, and a refrigerator seemingly parked in the middle of the floor plan, the couple thought they could do better.

"My notion was of a working kitchen where you can get in there and get things done—not pretty and fancy,

▲ **THE RUG** in the dining room came from Mark's previous condo and helped set the tone for the space: streamlined traditional in a modern gallery setting. Artwork includes two paintings by Christian Carlson, a sculpture and stand by Stashu Smaka, and a painting by Laurie Danial over the antique chest. A Nexus dining table by Altura Furniture is surrounded by a mix of discontinued chairs and two Bolier Domicile Crescent chairs; overhead is a Hampstead Caiman pendant lamp that echoes the shape of the footed Bose speakers.

Throughout the house, neutral and natural elements are emphasized. Textures of wood, glass, and metal play a key role in every room.

▼ **THE VIEW OF THE DINING ROOM** from the kitchen emphasizes its neutral and natural elements: wood, gray-stained masonry, the green outdoors view. Restrained touches of color include the cactus cachepot and a tile sculpture by Ken Shores in the corner.

more industrial," Mark says. "When I was younger and worked in restaurants as my livelihood, I became enamored with the idea that kitchens were not that different than a woodshop where you can beat it up a bit and that's OK."

The idea of a breakfast banquette was still appealing, but filtered through an architect's aesthetic it's a far cry from a red vinyl diner booth. Mark designed a custom wood table and an upholstered bench, with extra George Nakashima chairs that can be pulled up to seat six. And the room has other elements that are emblematic of '50s kitchens but are unabashedly modern in their implementation. For instance, the cabinet near the banquette has corner display shelves, and the open area above the cupboards serves much the same decorative purpose as the one in the "Retro Gem" chapter kitchen (see page 80). But the end result is far different.

The kitchen's beautiful walnut cabinetry and paneling are book-matched—the veneer is installed so that each piece is a mirror image of the one next to it—and all of that warm wood offsets the cool stainless steel appliances, counters, and backsplash. The double sinks are integral to the one-piece countertop, which was so large it had to be lifted by crane through the rear sliding-glass door. Most everything but the appliances is custom, including the central work island that Mark designed and a cabinetmaker built.

Was there some particular magic formula to its compact footprint? Not really—allowing for the necessary swing for the oven, dishwasher, and refrigerator doors, the remaining space is what he had to work with. "It's small but perfect; I like to be able to see utensils, not necessarily hanging from a rack, but more like on a tool caddy," he says.

One reason the Engbergs' kitchen is so pleasing is that Mark organized his design on sight lines present

▼ **A FLOS FUCSIA 3 LAMP** casts a glow on the surfboard-inspired breakfast table; there is hidden storage under the banquette seat and to the right of the dining area. The Nakashima chairs came from Design Within Reach. "The pottery I collect is contemporary," Laurie Engberg says. "I like the textures and that it's useful."

in the original architecture. "There are two datum lines that run through the entire first floor," he explains. "One is at the top of the low beams, which is the point where the ceiling springs away from the plane of the walls. The other datum is at the bottom of those same beams. These two imaginary lines are carried throughout; sometimes, as in the kitchen, they are both present in the design."

He points out that the open-box cabinets running along the ceiling mirror the height and depth of the beams, and the closed cabinets flanking the stove have a narrow reveal at that same line. The detail repeats in a ceiling display box in the hallway and in the new master bathroom, where the top of the mirror runs along the bottom datum line. It takes an architect to point out these organizational elements, but it makes things look seamlessly integrated and pleasing to the eye.

The couple took on the kitchen remodel simultaneously with the conversion of the attached garage to a master bedroom and bath—a five-month process during which they camped out downstairs. The 565-square-foot garage had been hyperbuilt to support the weight of two cars—the floor turned out to be solid 2x10s laid end to end—so carving a bedroom and large bath out of the space was fairly straightforward. A new stand-alone garage with a green living roof and an automobile turntable in the driveway were added at the same time.

Like the kitchen, storage in the bedroom and bath was a top priority. Walnut closets, drawers, and niches, as well as a shoji-style door, the bed frame, and nightstands were all custom-made by Neel Briggs of Big Branch Woodworking. In the bathroom, there's a walnut vanity and more custom cabinetry above the tiled wall opposite the sinks. The continuity of materials and design ties the three remodeled rooms together, as well as thematically to the rest of the house.

Mark does have a couple of second thoughts about the bath. Internal clerestories between the bath and bedroom would have brought more light into the dressing area, and both he and Laurie are dismayed by the

▶ THE GAGGENAU REFRIGERATOR was the only appliance that changed location, while a Bertazzoni stove, a Dornbracht faucet, and stainless steel counters, sinks, and backsplash by Custom Metal Fab are other new elements. "Stainless steel countertops are much more work than I thought they'd be," Laurie says, "but the floor is perfect for a kitchen: it can be really dirty and you can't tell."

The kitchen redesign melded cooking and dining areas, along with creating a hall leading to the new master bedroom and bath.

◄ **MAHOGANY BOARDS** were added to the front facade, and that same wood clads the new garage, the exterior of the bedroom balcony, and the deck off the living room. The driveway is now rain-permeable pavers and the James Bondian turntable flips the car around so the Engbergs don't have to back out into a blind intersection.

absorbency and staining of the concrete counter surrounding the sinks. Tackling the project today, it's likely Mark would have carried the mirror and tile to the top of the datum line instead of the bottom, but overall the master suite is a personal and functional success.

Two custom features of particular interest in this home are the stone flooring and the decorative screens; both demonstrate the subtle power of consistency. Seen next to the driveway, in the backyard, on the bedroom's shoji door, and in the entry hall, the screens are all riffs on a pattern routered into the original front door—although it's not an obvious ode to the casual observer.

"The design is not symmetrical, it's vertically oriented, yet has strong horizontal and interlocking lines," Mark explains. "The screens don't relate directly to the

◀ **A SHOJI SCREEN** slides over the glass door to the balcony for privacy, another usage of Mark's grid design seen outside the house and in the entry hall.

▲▶ **ORGANIZATION AND STORAGE** were key drivers behind the Engbergs' remodel. Because there's a place for everything, a custom bed, nightstands, and two Crate & Barrel cowhide ottomans are the

only furniture the bedroom needs. The floor has radiant heating, so it's a magnet for the couple's aging dog, Storm, and the padded vinyl headboard makes reading in bed a pleasure.

door, they don't look the same, but they have those same three characteristics."

Some screens are crafted from wood and some are metal; Mark made several personally, while Big Branch Woodworking and Stashu Smaka of Artisan Metalwork did others. Stashu fabricated the stairwell railing, the steel media storage unit, the frames around the new landscape window and the front door, and all of the pulls used on the custom cabinetry. A sculpture of Stashu's, a fine artist in his own right, even sits in the dining room.

The stone flooring is the first thing that catches your eye when you enter the house. The multicolor slate tiles appear again in the kitchen, but Mark clarifies that they are similar but not identical. Did they order two different tile brands? No; it's because each room's flooring was cut from 24" square slabs, and the entry and the kitchen were done several years apart. Individual tiles measure 4" wide by either 15.5" or 16" long; those dimensions were inspired by the 3" x 15" masonry units of the original fireplace, slightly modified to conserve saw cuts and the contractor's sanity. That kind of attention to detail is what makes an architect an architect.

The couple has now lived with the remodel for more than two years, and it's been five years since Laurie gave up her Foursquare in one of Portland's grand old neighborhoods. "I was such an Arts and Crafts person, but I love the openness and comfort of this house," she says. "We were listening to an NPR show that asked people if they could only save one thing, what would it be. Mark and I came up with the same answer at the same time: we'd save this house; it's really us."

▶ A 420-SQUARE-FOOT GARAGE was added when the original garage morphed into the master suite. The new structure has a flat, green roof that gives the uphill neighbors a garden view instead of looking at asphalt shingles. The balcony off the bedroom has the best vantage of the backyard, with landscaping by Organic Matters of Portland.

"I was
such an
Arts and
Crafts
person,
but I
love the
openness
and comfort
of this
house."

SPLIT-LEVEL, 1956
Cincinnati, Ohio
3,500 square feet
4 bedrooms, 3 baths

FAMILY MATTERS

A custom brick home gets a modern, child-friendly makeover that has evolved to stand the test of time.

◀ **OVERLEAF:** A black leather sectional, reissued Eames Wire Base tables, a Nelson Spindle clock on the fireplace wall, and an orange tray on the ottoman are all new purchases from Design Within Reach and Crate & Barrel. A green Bertoia Diamond chair is the vintage exclamation point in the arrangement, and a white and green rug from FLOR ties it and the predominately white dining area together. Glimpsed in the right foreground is a vintage Eames wire chair at the breakfast table in the open-plan kitchen.

▶ **JUST INSIDE THE FOYER,** the stairs to the right lead to the bedroom wing and walkout basement, while straight ahead is the living room. There's an interplay of light elements—walls and windows—and dark—floors and furnishings—throughout the house. A vintage Noguchi Cyclone table's chips and dings attest to its years of use, and prints by Charley Harper, a favorite midcentury Cincinnati artist, hang in the stair-well and in almost every room.

MODERN INTERIORS AND "FAMILY FRIENDLY" MIGHT SEEM MUTUALLY exclusive attributes, but Susan and Arlen Rissover's house shows that's not so. The couple, now in their late 40s, bought for the usual reasons—a good school district, enough bedrooms for their three kids, the acre lot—but insisted on midcentury modern architecture too.

"I remember being five years old and making my mother drive down certain streets to see the houses with the carports and flat roofs. I was always attracted to this architecture," says Susan, who specializes in modern real estate and founded a Cincinnati midcentury enthusiast group called cf3.

The living room is a good example of their style: it's painted white, has an expansive window wall looking out to the woodsy backyard, and the beamed ceiling and partition wall are natural redwood. The fireplace wall is brick, and there's handsome salt-and-pepper carpeting to physically and acoustically warm things up. Since the room dimensions are large—21' x 14'—the Rissovers have groupings of furniture that allow for traffic patterns to the foyer, family room, and bedroom wing.

▸ **THE CREDENZA IN THE CORNER,** the Florence Knoll–style end table, the Nelson bench by the window, and the graphic artwork by Emily Stewart and Charley Harper continue the rectilinear architecture theme—but then owners Susan and Arlen Rissover break it up. A curved sectional wraps around an oval Eero Saarinen pedestal coffee table and three Nelson bubble lamps are grouped in the corner, while a pair of Eames DCMs (dining chair, metal) are sculptural art you can use every day. All of these furnishings are vintage.

The architecture is all rectangles, from the windows and tongue-and-groove ceiling boards to the shape of the room itself.

"We first tried to make the living room all one cohesive space, but it just wasn't working—it was too big, so we separated it into two areas," Arlen says. "You can read or play music or sit and talk. It's my favorite room in the house—it has the most bling."

Near the bank of windows, a low bench that hits at sill height and doesn't block the eye connects the two ends of the room and their conversational groupings. Nestled against a wall with high clerestory windows, a curvaceous couch and ergonomic side chairs gather around a pedestal coffee table. There are multiple musicians in the family, and a piano is tucked next to the fireplace for practice sessions. In front of that, two Nelson Coconut chairs and an Isamu Noguchi coffee table make a great spot for a drink, with a warm fire at your back and a treetop view. None of their midcentury pieces are pristine after 20-odd years of cats and kids, but the couple takes that in stride.

FLOOR ME

MIDCENTURY HOMES HAD A VARIETY OF ORIGINAL FLOORING MATERIALS, depending on their style, era, and construction methods. Raised-foundation homes built in the late '40s and '50s with a basement or crawl space would often have hardwood in most rooms, sheet linoleum or asphalt or asbestos tile in the kitchen, and the same or ceramic tile in the baths. Later, when carpeting was king, plywood subfloors were covered with neutral wall-to-wall.

Sixties and '70s modernist homes built on cement slabs still had resilient tile in the wet rooms (and sometimes throughout), but added cork and poured terrazzo to the mix. Joseph Eichler used exposed aggregate and later ceramic tile in his entries, while custom houses sometimes had wood parquet, sealed brick, or 12" ceramic tile; by and large, flooring was meant to flow from room to room and be unobtrusive. Area rugs under furniture groupings, in bedrooms, and in front of the sink softened all those hard surfaces. (See pages 66, 89, and 159 for examples of re-created midcentury floors.)

Postwar buyers would have rarely considered concrete an appropriate finished floor surface, but exposing and polishing the original slab is a popular choice today. If you're dreaming of a pristine surface, though, think again: ghost outlines of tile mastic and mars from carpet tack strips are the norm, along with the hairline cracks that characterize mature concrete. Staining and sealing the cement, grinding and polishing, or floating a new self-leveling cement layer on top can disguise these problems. But all take an experienced pro and are expensive, so do lots of research before committing. If you have pets, fur tumbleweeds will show more than you ever dreamed, particularly on a dark floor.

Vinyl composition tile (VCT) is inexpensive and a close match for the original tile found in ranch homes; Armstrong and Azrock make lots of great patterns for both retro and contemporary looks. If you're a fan of stone, slate and terrazzo tiles lend themselves to modernist open-plan ranches, particularly those with concrete walkways or patios, like the example shown here. You'll note, too, that the more textured, colorful slate used in the homes in the chapters "Work of Art," "Crank Up the Volume," and "Artists' Collective" gives a much different look from the honed, gray squares seen in the chapters "Family Matters" and "On Tract."

Prefinished flooring, including cork or hardwood, is easy to install and less expensive, but in the experience of the homeowners we've met, those coatings don't hold up as well as site-finished materials. Bamboo is still proving its longevity claims, but my own pet peeve is wood-look laminate that sounds hollow when walked on and is nothing more than a photograph of wood applied to a sandwich of cellulose paper and plastic resin. This aptly fits Susan Rissover's definition of a "today" product that will look dated tomorrow.

Vinyl composition tile.

Slate and concrete meet at the front door.

Cork with a modern inlay detail.

The split-level floor plan combines openness with zoned activity—quiet bedrooms, a bustling kitchen, and multiple areas for entertaining.

◀ **IT'S THE LITTLE THINGS:** a $1 Nelson Ball clock, now at home in the downstairs family room, was the first midcentury piece the couple bought 25 years ago. Here, a second one hangs above the piano; to eliminate the cord, the Howard Miller Clock Company converted it to a battery movement. Notice how the shape of the Noguchi table echoes the triangle of the Coconut chairs, the latter bought for a $25 charitable donation from an office that was redecorating—one of the couple's biggest scores.

"Some people can be absolutely anal retentive about the tradition and perfection of modern furniture—just like people who collect baseball cards and comic books," Arlen comments. "We live with our stuff. Our Noguchi table got a chip in it from our daughter flipping over the ottoman to our Womb chair. And a friend dinged our Cyclone table when he was moving it. Things happen."

The house didn't look like it does today when they first found it, though. The sellers had put in acres of off-white plush carpeting, and there were ornate brass chandeliers, a grandfather clock, and drapes covering all of the windows. Built by local architect Fred Pressler for his own family, Susan suspects Mrs. Pressler might have had more traditional taste, and the home's original features reflected that. "It looked like the house was trying hard to be something it wasn't," Susan says.

When they bought 13 years ago, the Rissovers asked the sellers to take up the new carpeting and discovered that much of the house only had plywood subfloors. They made a quick decision to install hardwood in the family/dining room, kitchen, and stairs.

"I'm a big fan of continuous flooring—it makes spaces flow together and feel larger," Susan explains. "We made so many rushed decisions when we were moving in; the floor guy talked us into oak instead of maple because of the cost. But the finish didn't wear well, and when it needed redoing, we had them ebonized. I didn't realize it was a lot more work to keep dark floors clean."

The living room, bedrooms, and basement level got neutral Berber carpeting; later, the four bedrooms were upgraded to cork flooring, which is soft, warm, and both eco-friendly and midcentury appropriate. In the baths are gray slate tiles similar to those in the entryway, with retrofitted radiant heating underneath.

▲ **IN THE LOWER-LEVEL REC ROOM,** the Rissovers repeated some elements from upstairs: dark flooring—in this case, wall-to-wall carpeting—the vintage Saarinen pedestal table and chairs, a green Prince Aha stool, and a sculptural Bertoia Bird chair. The gray couch is from Design Within Reach and the coffee table is a vintage Eames design with a practical laminate top. The orange mat on the watercolor and the art glass on the table pick up the warm colors of the brick wall, which another owner might have painted, thinking it was too dark for a basement. If so, look how the continuity of materials would have been ruined as the wall continues past the glazing and out to the patio.

▲ **THE SCREENED PORCH** increases the home's footprint during temperate months. A dark rug Arlen Rissover cut into a curving amoeba shape anchors a Saarinen table surrounded by Bertoia chairs—all vintage and well loved. The CB2 mobile is a design element used in the stairwell, too, and the IKEA cachepots on the table parrot the shape of the stool by the sliding glass door.

There are two rooms for family TV watching, game playing, and hanging out—one in the walkout basement and the other adjacent to the kitchen—and both continue the theme of comfortable modern with dark sectional sofas and colorful vintage accent pieces like Diamond and Bird chairs designed by Harry Bertoia.

When they bought the house, the upstairs family room ceiling was drywalled and the beams were dark. The couple removed the drywall, installed skylights, and painted it all white. But the family room fireplace wall presented another aesthetic dilemma: Susan didn't love the brick and was tempted to cover it with stone. Luckily, she did nothing.

After living there for about six years, she met like-minded architects Chris Magee and Mike Keifling, who had ideas on how to modernize the white crown molding mantel and built-in that made Susan grind her teeth. "From day one, I wondered what the architect was thinking. We saw the listing sheet for the house when the original owners sold it, and the family room was done in Early American," she says in wonderment.

Chris and Mike designed a simple cherry mantel and a storage unit for the flat-screen TV and other media, plus two cantilevered display shelves that span the niche next to the fireplace. They chose cherry, funnily enough, because it matched the inexpensive IKEA credenza in the adjoining dining area. Suddenly, the brick worked just fine and Susan hasn't given another thought to covering it up.

In the other half of this same room sits a white dining set the couple bought 25 years ago. The midcentury-style table is surrounded with Series 7 chairs designed by Arne Jacobsen, while the pendant fixture that hangs overhead is by Poul Henningsen; all of these furnishings have traveled with them from home to home. Each is a classic midcentury design made of practical materials—laminate, bent plywood, chromed steel—and all three are still produced today.

Before they moved in, the Rissovers also remodeled the kitchen, widening the doorway between it and the family room. Rustic-looking original cabinets were structurally sound, so they were refaced with laminate and reconfigured slightly to accommodate a larger refrigerator, plus a cooktop and wall ovens in lieu of a range. Susan thought a white scheme would age well and chose Corian for the main countertops, with stainless steel on the island and laminate on the breakfast table. That kidney-shaped table was a custom feature they'd enjoyed at their previous home, so she duplicated it in a larger scale in this house.

◄▼ **IN THE DINING AREA,** a niche houses an IKEA buffet and wall cabinet that pick up the themes of white plus warm wood plus metal accents at play in the living room and adjacent kitchen. Because the space is just a touch larger than the credenza, and the same kitchen backsplash tile is used, the installation reads as a far pricier built-in. The oft-cited "Less is More" quotation is actually employed here: note the artful arrangement of the serving pieces behind the frosted glass, the decorative items limited to a mere three on the buffet—a Charley Harper print and stainless vessels by Jacobsen—and a Savoy vase by Alvar Aalto on the table. The laminate table has legs marked "Fritz Hansen," although the shape of the tabletop doesn't quite match Jacobsen's Super-Elliptical line for that company—yet another modern furniture mystery.

▲▶ **MORE THAN 10 YEARS OLD,** the kitchen bucks the stainless steel appliance trend with a refrigerator, range top, and wall ovens from Jenn-Air, an Asko dishwasher, and a GE microwave. The Modern Fan Co. ceiling fan and island countertop makes stainless steel an accent, not an era DNA marker. The custom breakfast table sits on a faux-Saarinen pedestal, a design motif that's duplicated in the genuine articles on the screened porch, in the basement family room, and in the living room. The chairs around it are vintage Eames.

Dark wood floors and stainless steel accents help make the white kitchen timeless rather than stark.

While saving money and time by refacing the cabinets, they splurged on some items like the Jacobsen-designed Vola faucet and Daltile's "Modern Dimensions" for the tile backsplash. A ceiling fan that's followed them from their last house and dark floors continue the calming white/black/metal palette; this allows them to freshen things up by changing the dishtowels, throw rugs, and accessories from time to time—a seasonal practice both architect Frank Lloyd Wright and designer Russel Wright promoted.

As a Realtor and ardent modernist, Susan has dispensed plenty of advice to new homeowners just embracing this aesthetic. "If there's something in your house that's in great condition, I always encourage people to keep it. If it's not there or not in good condition, I try to get into the mind-set of the original designer and think what they'd do if they had today's options," she explains.

▲ **THE BEDROOMS** are furnished with affordable modern pieces from Techline, items that have been in use for 10 years in some cases. Two vintage Bertoia chairs are in Kirsten's room, but everything else is pseudo built-in, which helps with crowd control in the modest-size space. Although the look is fun and bright, color is limited to green, orange, yellow, and a multicolor stripe repeated at the valance, the stretched art on the wall, and on the pillow slip and trundle mattress. The rectilinear elements are relieved by the curves of the Diamond chair, the green drawer pulls, the mobile in the corner, and the orange neck-roll pillow.

"Materials that are appropriate to the era are important; I don't like anything that looks like 'today,' because tomorrow it will look like yesterday and nobody wants that. For me, wow! factors include the creative use of tile—ceramic mosaic, not glass—cork floors, modern repro light fixtures like those from Remcraft, or you can rewire vintage fixtures. I think laminate and quartz countertops will stand the test of time, but granite is inappropriate in these older homes—it's so overdone and so expected in newer construction."

Arlen is also a Realtor, and his advice to midcentury design fans is even broader: "I tell people, if you collect modern furniture, you should live the modern life in a home like this. For one, the pieces look much better in that environment and, if you like the aesthetic that created those shapes, you'll like the space of a modern house," he enthuses. "The

▲ TENLEY'S ROOM
shares elements with her sister's space—the same cork floors and white laminate Techline pieces—but is individualized with a bed and storage bench from IKEA, a yellow/green/purple color scheme, and round FLOR area rugs. Susan designed the window seat, which was added along with the closet to its right; the room's original closet was annexed for the master bedroom, which shares a wall.

living rooms are bigger, the ceiling lines are higher, the windows are larger and let more light in. It's the perfect way to showcase your pieces. And when you find the right modern house for you, it just screams."

Some buyers might have screamed over the Rissovers' original bathrooms: the canted-front vanities have marble-patterned laminate counters that most folks would be itching to rip out, and the labyrinthine layout has a tub, two showers, two toilets, four sinks, and a dressing room all connected to the master bedroom.

"When we first looked at the house, I said, That's gotta go. But it's grown on me and it's very functional," Susan explains. "I love vintage bathrooms, but most die-hard modernists will have trouble with a pink bathroom. The more crazy laminates I see in various houses, the cooler I think they are now."

Slate floors in the baths helped unify the suite of wet rooms, and they all have plain white 4" x 4" tile as well. One thing Susan laments is that the original sinks have an unusual faucet hole configuration and hardware store fixtures had been installed. "I have looked for 12 years for American Standard replacements, including at building salvage yards," she says. "The chance of finding four that are in good condition is remote. The faucets we inherited are appropriate to the house, but they're not of a quality and a look that I would have chosen."

▲ **THE BATHS** illustrate typical period elements: metal rimmed sinks, wall-to-wall mirrors over the vanity, 4" field tile, and single-lever mixing taps; unique to the Rissover house are the wild laminate countertops that the family has come to appreciate. Many of the windows have vertical blinds and, while not a typical choice for this era of home, Susan cites seeing similar window coverings in a '50s interior design textbook and likes the light control and privacy they give.

▼ **THE MASTER BEDROOM** is cooler and calmer than the kids' rooms: the textured wall behind the Techline nightstands is painted a greenish neutral that coordinates with the Charley Harper artwork, the polka-dot pillow shams, and the FLOR carpet surrounding the bed. A vintage bench offers the punch of dark that we've seen employed upstairs, and $60 Ada table lamps from CB2 are simple and affordable. The Rissovers chose zebra cork from Eco-Friendly Flooring over the classic cork in the other bedrooms. "I don't do patterns lightly, but there's not a whole lot of jazzy stuff going on in our bedroom," Susan comments.

Arlen's favorite improvement to the house is actually just outside the front door—three floating concrete pads leading from the driveway that Susan dreamed up. "I didn't mind the brick pavers the house came with—they were a neutral; to me, replacing them wasn't worth the money and the effort at the time. But it was night and day what it does to the exterior of the house—and the exposed aggregate was my idea," he notes with a laugh.

"I think we enhanced and saved this house; it was a big, plain canvas when we bought it," Susan interjects. "I would hope that the original family would come back and be pleased with our taking it to the next level."

Arlen manages to get in the last beatific word: "Every morning I get up first and come down the hallway, go up the stairs into the foyer and I see the slate floor and the bullet planters, the light coming in and the kitchen beyond, and I think, Ah—I love that; our house is beautiful!"

▲ **THE VIEW** that greets Arlen every morning as he comes upstairs to put on coffee; the bedroom wing is behind the camera location, and the turn in the stairs leads down to the walkout basement. Initially the gold-color metal mesh on the stairwell was on the list for replacement, but architect Chris Magee suggested the Rissovers just spray it silver, and a can of Rust-Oleum did the trick. Bullet planters like the ones by the front door are available from Hip Haven or Design Within Reach.

▼ **MANY OF AMBERLEY VILLAGE'S ONE-ACRE LOTS** are beautifully wooded. The Rissovers' split-level home originally had a carport that has now been enclosed.

DEMONSTRATION RANCH, 1957

Brighton, New York
1,900 square feet
3 bedrooms, 2 baths

FULL METAL JACKET

Camouflaged as a plain-Jane ranch from the street, this aluminum kit house has amazing details to inspire, both inside and out.

▶ **THE PURPLE ALUMINUM PANELS** had been painted brown when the homeowners bought the house. "I read that they were supposed to have been anodized, but ours were factory painted and had faded," homeowner Steve Plouffe says. He took an unweathered panel off the garage to match the true color, and he and partner Mike Linsner spent more than a year painting them with a 2" brush. The grooved aluminum front and rear doors took a weekend each to strip, but today look as good as new.

**"OUR GOAL IS TO ENDOW THE HOME WITH A PER-
SONALITY**—delightful to be in, pleasant to live in, worthy of pleasure and
pride in possession," wrote architect Charles M. Goodman about a prototype '50s
house he designed for Alcoa. The company hoped the model would sweep the
nation in popularity; instead, only 26 were built. But, as the one that Steve Plouffe
and Mike Linsner live in reveals, the houses have personality to burn.

The "Care-free Home" was a hybrid between a demonstration house show-
casing an industry's bells and whistles—all-electric, steel-framed, or zero-
energy examples come to mind—and a kit-built house like a Sears bungalow or
porcelain-clad Lustron. Mike and Steve's ranch first arrived on a truck as 7,500
pounds of numbered components: siding, doors, wall panels, roofing, and the
termite shield were all made of aluminum, along with more traditional components like bricks, framing lumber, vinyl floor tile, and GE appliances. Although
the Alcoa experiment was not a commercial success (the builder of this house
ended up living in it for 25 years when it proved too expensive and unusual to sell),
the upstate New York house is as well built and carefree as its brochure boasted.

"Anything that's clad in aluminum never has to be painted; you just wipe it
down," Steve, 45, says. "It has a lifetime roof and the cypress, redwood, and
walnut walls and ceilings are pretty carefree—you don't have to do anything to

**THE ALCOA
HOUSE** near Rochester
has the same floor plan as
others built in 16 different states. As the original
brochure shows, the details
and materials are what set
it apart.

those." Because the Alcoa house was built with double-pane windows and aluminum surface insulation, he reports that utility bills are on par with those at their last place, an '80s builder house. "Relative to a conventionally constructed house that's 50 years old and never had anything done to it, this home is in much better shape."

The front facade has some wild elements that invite a double take the first time you visit: purple exterior panels, decorative blue grillwork on the windows, and greenish-gold doors, all fabricated from aluminum. A simple side-gable ranch with pierced-brick privacy walls is transported to Wonderland—or at least Sinatra's Las Vegas—with these colorful period embellishments.

Inside, the posts and beams and the wood wall sections—all built on a 12' grid—are edged in aluminum, which gives a crisp, tailored appearance to the midcentury house. Other walls are anodized aluminum panels trimmed with wood furring strips, while doors on the numerous built-ins are bold-colored laminate or textured aluminum. It's easy to see how the builder was able to charge $1 a head for a tour of this futuristic house back in the day.

The couple knew they were lucky to find such a distinctive jewel box and that it deserved equally singular furnishings; fortunately many of their existing pieces made the grade. Yes, they have some of the usual suspects—a Saarinen Womb chair, Eames plywood chairs, a couple of Heywood-Wakefield pieces, a Barcelona chair—but by selecting from a broader midcentury menu and curating their accessories and art, Steve and Mike have created an exceptional interior, although neither is a trained designer.

▲ **A LESSON FOR ALL OF US** tempted to toss original elements that don't appeal to our personal aesthetic: the curvy laminate telephone desk was found in the basement and reinstalled in the hall near the back door, where it began life. Teamed with a modern-made Norman Cherner chair with turquoise cushions, it makes this corner sing.

▶ **FROM THE FRONT DOOR,** you step into a small foyer with built-in closets, seen just beyond the two black Eames molded plywood chairs. Immediately, the drama of the open-plan architecture is revealed. A Square Dance rug from FLOR is inset into a recess in the original vinyl floor, a feature designed to make vacuuming easier that's repeated elsewhere in the house.

Color and pattern are confined to artwork, pottery, and glass, and even the single pillow on the couch adheres to the scheme.

▲ **THE HORIZONTAL PANELING AND WINDOW GRILLE** form a textured background for a striking vignette: a Robert Ernst Marx painting is lit by a Tolomeo floor lamp, and an Eileen Gray table holds a colorful ceramic sculpture by Bill Stewart. The Barcelona chair, newly purchased from Knoll, is paired with a knock-off ottoman for now, but the couple wants to make the set complete.

For instance, the living room is about as graphic as it gets: carpeting is usually a background neutral, but here oversize brown and tan circles—a warmer color combo that still reads as black and white—command the room and play off the paintings over the white vintage sofa. The homeowners continue the theme with five black chairs: the two Eames LCWs, two Marcel Breuer B35 loungers, and the Ludwig Mies van der Rohe–designed Barcelona.

The tables have chrome frames, as do several of the chairs, and glass or marble tops. Color and pattern are confined to artwork, pottery, and glass, and even the single pillow on the couch adheres to the scheme. In the view toward the front door, it's easy to see why this living room needs a minimalist approach: the lavender and blue aluminum wall panels and greenish front door bring plenty of visual excitement.

The house came with a copy of the vintage Alcoa brochure, and one option would have been to replicate the furnishings it showed. "That was a little too casual for me," Mike, 50, says. "The house had a Mies van der Rohe or Le Corbusier feel to it I thought, especially in the living room. I wanted to go a little more modern."

"Metal and leather, rather than wood and fabric," Steve translates. "There was enough wood on the ceilings and walls."

The dining room is at the base of the U-shaped open plan; it has a bare floor in summer, but the couple also puts down a red Oriental rug during the winter. For as airy a look as possible, they chose a reissued

▶ **THE LIGHTING** in the living room includes a no-name eBay lamp on the round Eileen Gray table by the sofa, and an interesting vintage pendant made of capiz shell that came with the house. The marble-topped end table is a Knoll and the large glass vases are by David Thai. A $50 sofa reupholstered in white with crisp piping appears traditional yet modern; just think how different it would look in a floral or stripe. Two '70s paintings by Kay Stowell are over the couch— slightly different widths, you'll notice, which gives the installation some nice tension—and the bust on the Knoll coffee table is by Robert Ernst Marx.

In contrast to the living room, the dining room exploits pops of color, setting the style for the rest of the house.

Dining area

In the Alcoa Care-free Home the light, bright dining area is sensibly situated between living and family rooms and still only a step from the central kitchen.

Rich panels of walnut framed by smart yet functional Care-free aluminum provide a tasteful backdrop on one side, while the other is a wall of glass with aluminum sliding doors opening onto the adjacent terrace. Outside, overhead lighting keeps the glass area from becoming a black mirror after nightfall. There's plenty of light inside, too, from recessed aluminum lighting fixtures.

◄ THE METAL AND GLASS TABLE was designed in 1928, but it looks quite at home with the fiberglass '60s Ion chairs by industrial designer Gideon Kramer. Overhead, a Nelson cigar lamp is a reissue purchased at Design Within Reach. The Alcoa brochure shows the reverse view of a Care-free Home dining room outfitted with Danish Modern, which was a little too casual for the homeowners.

the Care-free kitchen

Mother can see and be seen by her family in this bright, efficient kitchen "control center," overlooking both family room and dining area. Equipment and floor plan combine to save steps and lighten chores as well.

Laminated plastic counter tops are just the right height to minimize bending. Range, oven, dishwasher, waste disposal unit and wall-hung refrigerator are all built in and aligned in step-saving sequence to make food preparation easier. There's light galore from aluminum fluorescent fixtures and overhead spots to cover every inch of work space and cabinet interiors, too. And ductless ventilation instantly whisks away every trace of cooking odors. There is a wealth of storage cabinets.

the Bathrooms

Colorful, spacious twin bathrooms are just a step away from the bedrooms.

Polyethylene diffusers make the entire ceiling a source of light to bathe the room. Wall panels of moistureproof laminated plastic and glass tub enclosure are both framed in aluminum for enduring good looks. Clean-up chores involve no more than the whisk of a damp cloth.

▶ THE NEW KITCHEN resembles the original shown in the '50s brochure: the sink and cooktop are in similar positions, though the metal cabinets have been reconfigured and the wall-hung refrigerator (on the left wall in the brochure's vintage view) abandoned as impractical. This room is all about rectangles—the expanse of new sheet vinyl on the floor, the Corian counters, the original fluorescent fixture overhead, and the blocks of color seen in the upper and lower cabinets and backsplash. The far walls are papered in pale grass cloth.

Le Corbusier LC6 table and Ion chairs found at an online vintage site. These continue the usage of metal but add in more pops of color as you transition to the kitchen and lounge.

The kitchen came to them with '70s oak cabinets, a standard refrigerator and range, a hulking pantry cupboard, and laminate counters; it was narrow, dark, and had little to recommend it. While some of the home's original metal cabinets were found in the garage, re-creating the 1957 space with its wall-hung GE refrigerator seemed impractical. "We were looking for something that suggested the '50s but had more modern conveniences," Steve says.

The pair, both software engineers, used the original Care-free Home brochure for kitchen inspiration, including the placement of the appliances. "We wanted to keep it as simple as possible and use materials that were manufactured; granite countertops didn't make sense," Mike says. "This is a prefab house and that's not something that they would have used. We weren't looking for boomerang laminate or something exactly period, yet we didn't think a sleek, Euro kitchen would be appropriate."

The metal cabinets were sprayed blue at a body shop and hung on both sides of the galley kitchen; a custom stainless steel hood for the range top was fabricated to span the width of the cabinets and provide task lighting. "We looked for lower cabinets that were simple, with flat fronts. The best we could find happened to be the cheapest—IKEA Akurum in

▶ **IF THE HOMEOWNERS**

had opted to close the pass-through or gone with a solid wall of cabinets, the flow and aesthetics of both the kitchen and the lounge would have been marred. The blue, white, green, and black laminate–faced storage unit is original to the Alcoa house, and by choosing complementary but not strictly matching colors in the new kitchen, it all works as a piece. A reissued Noguchi Cyclone table sits between the Heywood-Wakefield Ladies' Club chairs, and the cabinet tops hold some of the couple's ceramics collection.

Applad black," Mike explains. "In our past houses, we've installed kitchens with very expensive Wood-Mode cabinets, and we like the IKEA cabinets just as well. Since the space was a fairly standard 12' x 8', stock cabinets fit perfectly."

Counters are white Corian, a material they like to think would have been used in the '50s if it had existed. A Wolf range top, Frigidaire oven, Bosch dishwasher, and Kohler sink were other selections. Although a Sub-Zero would have fit the shallow counter depth perfectly, they decided to use the existing refrigerator until it stops working; the trash compactor was retained as well. Lime green backsplash tiles tie in with the colorful cabinets in the lounge, just on the other side of the pass-through.

"All in all, this has turned out to be our favorite kitchen—and the least expensive, costing under $8,000 to redo," Mike reports.

The public rooms wrap around this central kitchen, and each area, while open to the others, has its own feel. Without walls to demarcate the dining room or the den, it can be tricky to arrange furniture groupings that work when viewed from both sides. One area where they ran into this issue was in the lounge.

CONTEMPORARY KITCHENS

CLEAN DESIGN AND AN ECONOMICAL PRICE POINT make a modern IKEA kitchen hard to resist, but there are other options. This room should work in the context of your home's architectural style—whether it's a modernist or "granny" ranch—so if your house or taste points to a kitchen that looks like it's straight out of *Mad Men*, flip to "Vintage Kitchens" on page 90.

While it's tempting to include all of the latest trends in a remodel, resisting that will help keep your kitchen from looking dated in 20 years; trust me, avocado and harvest gold appliances were cutting-edge in their day. Instead, look to examples like the Case Study and Eichler homes, or the Engbergs' kitchen on page 25 for an understated, elegant modernism that will better stand the test of time. Hard-edge, glossy, high-end Euro kitchens are a better fit for new construction, in my opinion.

Cabinetry If the original cabinets are in good condition but not "you," consider repainting the bodies and installing new hinges and modern pulls; often the vintage construction is of superior quality to what you can buy today and you'll give the next owners the option to restore them. If the doors are shot, the boxes may still be sound, and you'll save a ton of money compared to starting completely over; the homeowners in the chapter "Family Matters" (page 46) and the chapter "Crank Up the Volume" (page 112) chose this approach.

But if you need all-new cabinets, consider the laminate and plywood line from Kerf, which includes midcentury touches such as sliding doors with finger holes, display niches, and decorative vents on the sink apron. For more premium budgets, Henrybuilt has some beautiful options that speak to modern and vintage sensibilities with their credenza-like islands and natural woods.

Counters IKEA, Wilsonart, Formica, and other companies sell laminate for countertops in myriad solid colors. Widely used on iconic modern furniture and in '60s kitchens, it looks just right and is durable and carefree if you avoid hot pots and knife cuts. Other good choices include stainless steel and solid surface materials with 90-degree edges that approximate the look of laminate (at a much higher price point). But please eschew granite and marble—they have no place in a postwar home.

Appliances Scale is important in the ranch kitchen. Instead of a six-burner, restaurant-grade stove with stainless steel backsplash and oversize hood dominating a small space, a cooktop and wall oven will keep your kitchen more authentic looking. Thermador and Westinghouse were among the appliance lines chosen for these houses when they were new, and they and Electrolux have models that are a bit smaller and more in tune with the unpretentiousness of these homes. As a plus, they're often more affordable too.

Kerf's cabinetry melds midcentury and contemporary aesthetics.

The brochure's floor plan shows the built-ins and smart organization of the Alcoa Care-free Home.

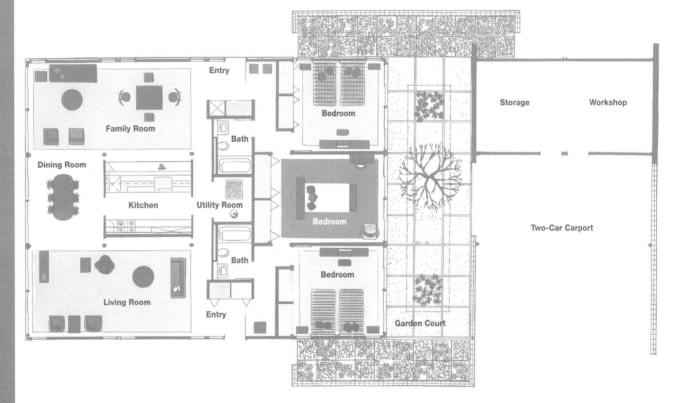

Entry

Family Room

Dining Room

Kitchen

Utility Room

Bath

Bath

Living Room

Entry

Bedroom

Bedroom

Bedroom

Garden Court

Storage

Workshop

Two-Car Carport

▼ **THE HEYWOOD-WAKEFIELD PIECES**—the club chairs and the painted round table—the Florence Knoll credenza, and many of the decorative period flourishes were purchased on craigslist or at local vintage stores. The modular carpeting is from FLOR, and note the metal detailing: aluminum frames the tongue-and-groove wood walls and ceiling, and demarcates the floor registers (in front of the windows). The legs on the credenza and the Laurel floor lamp continue that metal theme, first seen in the living room, while simultaneously emphasizing the warmer wood here in the lounge.

Forming the second long side of the U, the lounge mirrors the size of the living room. It has a darker, clubbier feel, and a bit funkier furnishings. Mike tends to be lead dog on home improvements, but Steve was the one who found the two vintage daybeds and Lane tables on craigslist; his partner was less than enamored with the selections. Stepping in to save the day was Josef Johns, a friend and interior designer who suggested re-covering the couches in purple linen.

"This is no ordinary ranch house," says Josef, who typically works in a more traditional style on Victorian homes and was not in love with the house initially. "Everything about its design—the logical disposition of spaces, the contrast of gleaming surfaces with warm woods, the comfortable mixture of coziness and grandeur—places the house in a class by itself. And then there is the fact of its being perfectly symmetrical; that's what really won me over."

Josef's choice of color for the upholstery and the iridescent silk curtains lining the window walls relates to the nearby aluminum closet doors, as well as the blazing purple panels on the exterior. Teamed with two Heywood-Wakefield armchairs in a nubby grayish boucle, vintage lamps, and a killer starburst mirror, the reupholstered pieces and the room work wonderfully for parties.

The bedrooms are larger than those in many other ranches, but all three have a wall of glass that opens to a private courtyard—a nice amenity, but it does limit furniture placement. The key to making it work is the built-in clothes storage behind bifold aluminum doors and, in the master bedroom (a mere three feet longer than the other two bedrooms), additional cupboards in the clerestory area over the closets.

A bed, wenge wood dresser used as a headboard, and chair are all that the master bedroom needs. Good thing, because the area between the closet and bed functions as a mini-hall, with doors leading to the adjoining bedrooms. In addition to '50s and '60s paintings by local artists—an earlier collecting obsession of Mike's—the decor is dominated by an oversize houndstooth-patterned carpet and a handsome tailored bedspread suggested by Josef.

▶ THE ORIGINAL **ALCOA BROCHURE** showed a bath with laminate walls outlined in aluminum channeling. For the 2010 version, the homeowners bought white laminate sheets at a big-box store, cut them to size with a razor blade and straightedge, and finished the imperfect edges with heat-affixed black laminate tape. The grid begins with the original illuminated ceiling and includes dark blue sections in the corners. The commode and sink are Duravit's Foster suite, which includes a siphon cover that pretties up the under-sink pipes and supply handles; a similar toilet for small spaces is Toto's Aquia. Still searching for the perfect towel bar, for now they use temporary hooks on the dry end of the shower.

"Another friend offered to make it for us," Mike says about the coverlet. "It turned out to be very complicated and took many, many hours to make, but we think it was worth the effort—although our friend who made it may not agree."

A guest bedroom is outfitted with red FLOR carpet squares and a patterned spread on the West Elm platform bed. Behind it is a substantial custom wenge wood headboard made for their previous home, and a four-panel painting that set the color scheme for the room. In the third bedroom, used as an office, a vintage Florence Knoll couch and a new Bertoia Diamond chair offer a place to relax. Green modular carpet is in this room, and coordinating drapes were recently added at the sliding glass door.

The designer also helped Steve and Mike focus their ideas for a bathroom remodel. Both baths had been generically updated in the '80s with big-box fittings and the pair wanted to riff on the original design but with modern fixtures. They liked that the Alcoa brochure showed a wall-hung toilet and laminate panels (see page 66), but they opted for a marble-clad shower stall instead of a tub.

Josef sketched a Piet Mondrian–like grid of laminate wall panels that the couple cut, mounted, and outlined with black tape themselves. A custom recessed medicine cabinet—the same width as the panel, you'll note—and barber pole–style vanity lights complement the original polyethylene ceiling fixtures.

"The toilet with the tank in the wall provided an extra foot of space and, along with the sink being hung from the wall, makes the 5' x 8' bathroom seem much larger," Steve explains. "The shower has a simple piece of glass separating it from the rest of the room, and its floor is level with the main bathroom floor, which allowed us to use the same 12" marble tiles on the floor and shower walls. And the oversized medicine cabinet is extra deep because of the space behind the wall used for the toilet tank; this works out well because there's no other storage in the room."

Their second bath was remodeled after our shoot. The original tub and ceiling light fixture were retained, and a slightly different wall-hung toilet and sink from the Duravit line were chosen, along with gray 6" square glass tile on the walls and a linoleum floor with an inlaid starburst—contemporary, yet in keeping with the era of the home.

"Before we moved in, people thought we were crazy to buy it," Mike says. "But after we cleaned everything up and put in our furniture, they started to understand it. People couldn't even imagine how you would arrange furniture here; now everyone says they love it."

Then there are the comments from random neighbors: "People always want tours," Steve reports with a smile. "We hear things like, 'It's so much nicer than I thought driving by!'"

▸ **THE INSET CARPET AREAS** in the various rooms ensure that the ratio of textiles to resilient flooring remains consistent and in scale with the home. Too often homeowners skimp on area rugs and the resulting furniture groupings look like they're huddled on a postage stamp. In the guest bedroom, the painting over the bed is by Mick Park and the 1955 Eames wire mesh rocking chair still has its original seat pad. All three bedrooms have sliding glass doors that lead to a garden patio between the garage and house, with brick privacy walls on each end.

TRADITIONAL RANCH, 1955

Tulsa, Oklahoma
2,200 square feet
3 bedrooms, 2 baths

RETRO GEM

Built as a model home for a tract, this quintessential ranch showcased a variety of brick, man-made stone, and modern fixtures.

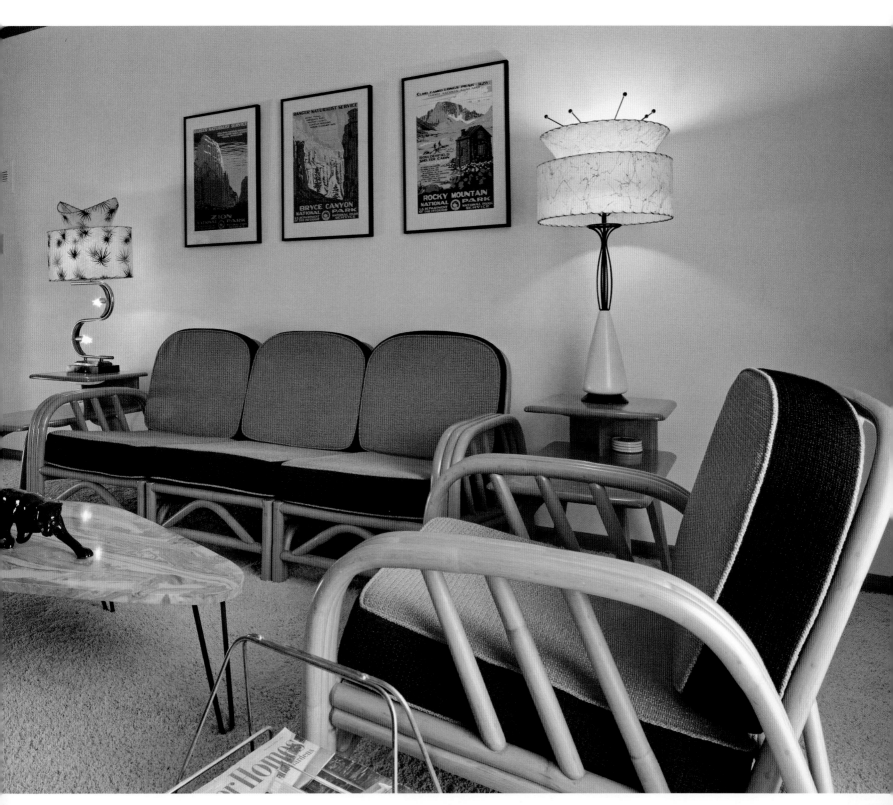

◀ **OVERLEAF:** In the living room, Jennie Hall has combined a vintage bamboo couch and chair with two Heywood-Wakefield side tables and a poured resin surfboard-style coffee table with hairpin legs. The travel posters and colorful upholstery work best in this room, with its new neutral carpeting, but the Halls plan to exchange the seating once they find the right sectional sofa.

▶ **THE ORIGINAL CABINETS,** with their warm though not pristine finish, are the major style-setters in the kitchen. Vintage Homecrest barstools and the black components on the Frigidaire cooktop and spice set give the room some grounding that bright upholstery and shiny chrome would not, while the brushed stainless steel dishwasher front ties in with the metal knobs and original appliances. Jennie loves to thrift, and her collection of canisters, Hall ceramics, and Pyrex bowls are both useful and evocative of the period.

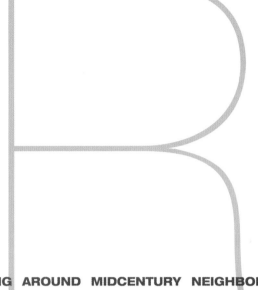

RIDING AROUND MIDCENTURY NEIGHBORHOODS WITH REALTOR ALYSSA STARELLI, SHE'LL WAX rhapsodic about the "granny ranches" that fly right under most folks' cool-house radar. You know, the ones that look like they're straight out of *Leave It to Beaver,* with a scalloped wood valance over the kitchen sink, pink and aqua tile in the bath, and a knotty pine bar in the basement rumpus room. The kind of time-capsule houses that give lots of people hives—but not Alyssa, and not Jennifer and Johnney Hall, the owners of a typical ranch in Tulsa.

Their kitchen is the perfect place to start the time-machine tour. From the turquoise laminate counters and long-oak cabinets to the coppertone range hood and aqua rotary wall phone, the Halls' house epitomizes '50s originality. Two electric burner units flip closed when not in use, and a motor that powers a knife sharpener, mixer, and blender is built right into the counter. In the large room—roughly 15' x 17'—the cabinetry forms an L, while a glass display case next to the dining area functions as a room divider. Opposite the cooking area a brick alcove holds the wall oven, a planter with plastic foliage, and a built-in pole lamp. To its left, behind louver doors, is a full-on bar with lockable liquor compartments.

But Jennie, 33, and Johnney, 38, aren't retro purists who live a *Pleasantville*-type lifestyle. In fact, the house is an amalgam of original elements, modern appliances, and laboriously re-created midcentury details. In the kitchen, a new dishwasher sits next to the corner-mounted turquoise sink, and the oven is a recent Frigidaire model. A wall-mounted turquoise refrigerator (similar to the one in the Alcoa house brochure, page 66) originally hung to the left of the sink, but previous owners

▶ ALTHOUGH THE WALL-HUNG REFRIGERATOR is gone, this view of the kitchen looks virtually the same as in 1955. The original wallpaper is visible here and may guide the homeowners' replacement pattern. The faded, nubby turquoise curtains are original as far as the Halls can tell, and preservation-minded Jennie plans to take them down and store them in a box for the next owners.

replaced it with cabinets; now a stainless steel side-by-side is tucked next to the washer and dryer in a corner.

The smaller scale of '50s appliances can make them difficult to replace. The Halls wished that the home's original turquoise wall oven and dishwasher had survived, but since they'd already been supplanted with '70s models, they opted for new ones. And because the location of the refrigerator wasn't original to the floor plan, that also offered challenges.

▼ **THE COPPERTONE RANGAIRE EXHAUST HOOD** appears to be original, but the avocado wall oven and refrigerator that were in place when the house was purchased were later additions. Folding Frigidaire burners were manufactured by General Motors and, near the blue Hobart mixer, a NuTone in-counter motor powers several small appliances. The edge of the counter bears a scar from a larger dishwasher, and the Sputnik fixture over the sink is a recent addition.

"We had to chisel out an inch of brick to make the
new oven fit, and the refrigerator was hard to find, too,"
says Jennie, who's a library paraprofessional. "We
needed a side-by-side to work in the narrow corridor,
and most were too big and too tall; same thing with
the washer and dryer." Since their flip-up burners are
brushed chrome, the Halls felt stainless steel coordi-
nated the best and found everything they needed in the
Frigidaire line.

Several renovation ideas were sparked by black-
and-white photos and a 1955 Parade of Homes brochure that the sellers passed along. These revealed
that the Halls' ranch was a model home for builder
Lloyd Creekmore's development. Designed by Don
Rector, its modern amenities included a Westinghouse
appliance center, a Melody Queen radio/intercom (even
in the baths), four kinds of brick or man-made stone,
an indoor grill, and Sputnik and other futuristic light
fixtures—all features that sang to the Halls when they
toured it in 2005.

The house did have a couple of not-so-great
updates, though: brightly colored carpets and cot-
tage cheese–textured ceilings gave them pause. Since
thoughtful decisions are the couple's style, they lived
with screaming teal plush in the family room and living room, and beat-up sheet vinyl in the kitchen until

▶ DOGBONE CHAIRS
surround a Heywood-Wakefield
wishbone table made in 1949, and
the coral dishes are vintage Russel
Wright American Modern. Overhead is a Nelson saucer bubble
lamp. In the background you can

see the brick alcove that houses
the oven and pole lamp, and
beyond that the new refrigerator.
The sellers told Jennie that when
they hung the wallpaper in the
kitchen, they made a template for
the built-in clock numbers so they
could put it all back perfectly.

▼ **THE VIEW FROM THE DINING AREA** shows the foyer with its original Sputnik wall lamp and built-in planter, looking much the same as it did in 1955. Three mahogany and brass sculptures of performing seals are on the fireplace surround; Jennie has seen a duck version used on the set of *Mad Men*. Sometime in the past a bookcase was added; to its right is a glimpse of the living room.

recently. Now a two-tone vinyl composite tile floor runs from the kitchen into the dining and family room, and the living room has neutral wall-to-wall shag.

"We pulled up the carpet in the family room and found the original tiles," Johnney explains. "A lot of them were in fantastic shape so we wondered if there was any way we could get matching ones to replace the broken pieces. But in the end, the carpet strips had caused too much damage."

"For some reason, the first owners had replaced the original tile in the kitchen," Jennie adds. "It was hard to decide if we wanted cork or VCT or some kind of stone. Then we wondered if we should do tile in the '50s light and dark brown colors, or go with something new. It seemed like brown didn't really go with anything else in the house: the fireplace brick is kind of pinkish and the wood paneling is a different shade of brown. So we decided on white and turquoise, but in the original diagonal striped pattern."

"Jennie vacillated between the white and blue and the browns," says Johnney, who's a computer programmer. "She thought about playing it safe and even tried to hybridize the two schemes by bringing a brown stripe into the mix."

"That was because there was also the question of what color carpet would go with the floor," Jennie explains. "I didn't think we wanted bright white carpet in the living room."

With all of the paneling and the wood ceilings, Johnney's vote was for something light colored, which he felt would make the space look bigger. "Jennie even had a poll going on her blog about which color combination looked best. In the end, I told her she should just go with her gut."

"Autumn Haze [a light tan] was the tasteful choice," Jennie concludes. "But I said, 'Let's get wild!'" Johnney interjects.

He called Tulsa's environmental quality department to make sure they could remove the original tile themselves without needing asbestos abatement. "The guy said I could go ahead and pull it up—that any asbestos would be stuck in the tile matrix. He advised us to just take it up piece by piece and, if you wanted to be really safe, wet it down first." Luckily, most tiles were loose and could be removed whole; the process took all of 20 minutes.

But they weren't so fortunate with the kitchen flooring demo. "The first pass, we got the vinyl off the backing," Johnney recounts. He then scored the paper backing and softened it with acetone. That left the mastic. "It was vile. We found an adhesive remover from Ace Hardware, and would take a 2' x 3' square and let the remover sit on it, then just scrape and scrape until it was clean." He estimates it took a couple of hundred hours. Did we mention the Halls launched this project with the *Atomic Ranch* photo shoot looming?

"If we can do it, we will," says Jennie about their DIY approach.

In addition to the checkerboard floor, the old photos inspired punchy window coverings. Jennie found barkcloth drapes—some vintage and some reproduction fabrics—which she altered and installed in the dining room, bedrooms, and one bath. Bold elements like these mean other patterns have to be kept to a minimum; their family room's Philippine-mahogany walls and neutral blond wood furniture fit the bill.

▶ **THE AZROCK TILE FLOOR** in "Cirrus" and "Spearmint" and the barkcloth drapes were inspired by the original photo; the Halls may have similar area rugs made in the future. Jennie bought the coral chair in the family room for $30 when she was a teenager, and the tables are Heywood-Wakefield. The $10 sectional was found at an estate sale in the neighborhood, but it was in such poor condition that it took Jennie all day to convince her husband it was worth the upholstery investment.

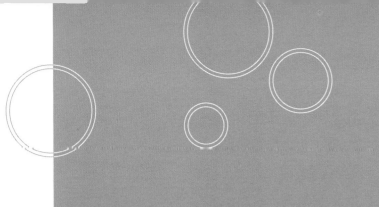

VINTAGE KITCHENS

AN AUTHENTIC KITCHEN IS ALL ABOUT THE DETAILS, from the flooring to appliances to the light fixtures on the ceiling. While many house-hunters would find such a room dated, retaining or re-creating a midcentury kitchen can be the highlight of a home.

Look at period photos and drawings in old magazines and books for a good feel for the right elements, or go to retrorenovation.com. A kitchen in a traditional '50s ranch might have corner display shelves and a pass-through to the dining room, while a more modernist '60s house will emphasize furniture-like cabinets well suited to an open floor plan. A kitchen that fits the style of the home, like the Halls' or the one in the chapter "Minimalist Masterpiece" (page 184), feels exactly right and gives you pleasure every day.

Appliances   Whether you gravitate to vintage stoves and refrigerators or retro-look appliances like those from Big Chill and Elmira Stove Works (Northstar refrigerator, right), these items will dictate the room's authenticity. Reconditioned 1950s stoves such as those from O'Keefe & Merritt are readily available, but refrigerators and '60s electric ovens and range tops in great condition are much harder to find. Craigslist or enthusiast boards can be a good place to find a still-working appliance that needs a new home; just be aware that it may take dedication to find parts and a repairman to service them. And branch out of today's stainless steel ghetto: a blue retro fridge to match your '50s wall oven, or a red stove that coordinates with original counter tile may not be safe, but what fun is playing it safe?

Cabinetry   Unfortunately, few cabinet manufacturers make styles that approximate what was originally in your home. These were usually birch or maple veneer, knotty pine, or paint-grade wood with flat doors, or of all-metal construction like those in the Alcoa house (page 67), or "Minimalist Masterpiece" (page 184). If they're still in place, consider keeping them; if they've already been removed, look to your neighborhood or online for entire kitchens being removed by unappreciative owners. Cabinets can be refinished or painted, sprayed at an auto body shop if metal, and dressed with new or vintage knobs and pulls. Deciding to demo your cupboards will almost always lead to a full-gut remodel.

Counters   Laminate comes in retro patterns such as "cracked ice" or boomerang, with or without metal edging. Another good choice is 4" ceramic tile—with thin grout lines, please, unless you want to channel the '80s. Either option should have a matching backsplash. One material on the counter and another on the backsplash is a current trend that will surely fade, and we're aiming for continuity and an edited number of elements that look as though they could be original.

Wall Coverings   Consider wallpaper, either on a wall without cabinets, in the soffit area like in the Halls' kitchen, or a border running along the ceiling, to give your room '40s and '50s charm without adding too much visual noise. Both vintage-look and actual period papers are available online from sites like Bradbury & Bradbury ("Atomic Doodle," middle right), Rosie's Vintage Wallpaper ('60s op art, top right), and Secondhand Rose. Once you select a paper, picking up one or two of its colors for paint, knobs, textiles, or collectibles can really pull the room together.

A traditional ranch like this one lends itself to modest, era-appropriate upgrades instead of slick, contemporary finishes.

Porch

Kitchen Dining

Office Bath Master Bedroom

Family Room

Bath Guest Bedroom

Garage Living Room

◀▼ **PINK POODLE TIME:**
Jennie's thrifting habit, born when she was a kid, is fully in evidence in the master bedroom. The vanity area has a marbleized laminate counter, similar to those at the home in the chapter "Family Matters" (see pages 49–50), a Heywood-Wakefield Sculptura stool, and a Westinghouse record player. Off camera is a cubby for the then-cutting-edge bedroom TV set. "It has a switch plate by the bed for those pre-remote days," explains Jennie. "The original remote-control system was a light switch," Johnney laughs.

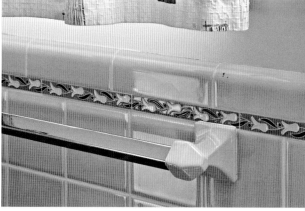

The home's exterior is a combination of traditional and midcentury zing—the beige man-made-stone facade, shake-look roof, and aluminum windows get a kick from the red, center-knob front door and the wrought-iron porch supports. Wisely, the Halls picked up the red accent color on the garage door without going overboard. Inside it's much the same: as modern as the '50s electric kitchen and soaring family room ceiling were, the bedrooms and baths would have been comfortable and familiar to most middle-class postwar buyers. Or at least one of the baths.

The smaller of the two is pink, pink, pink. The sink sits on chrome legs, a style that preceded wall-hung models, and the toilet is a classic '40s/'50s model. The original 4" tile is in great shape and, between the built-in TP holder, towel bars, and flower-motif accent tiles, you have to admire the flourishes the builder put into this master suite bath.

The room was less attractive when they bought the house: a brown sink had replaced the original, but they found this pink one on eBay. Trouble was, the seller lived in New Jersey and it and a matching toilet were "Local pickup only" items. But Johnney sweet-talked the owner into shipping the pair, so now the Halls have a spare toilet should theirs expire. "eBay is the boon of preservationists everywhere," Johnney says.

As modern as the '50s electric kitchen was, this bath would have been comfortable and familiar to most middle-class postwar buyers.

▼ THE GRAY BATHROOM, after it was freed from inappropriate remodeling, looks very close to its 1955 appearance, save the psychedelic wallpaper. Applied moldings obscured the vents on the vanity, and since the Zolatone finish had been painted over, the Halls gave it a coat of black and added new pulls. The faucets are new, while the half-century-old tile just looks new.

Down the hall is a second gray and black bath that also has 4" field tile with a decorative trim, but that's where the similarity ends. Twin sinks are built into a slant-front cabinet, and a tile half wall next to the toilet houses a planter and what can only be described as a planetary room divider. Two ceiling fixtures continue that theme with space-age design elements. The walls have some wild '70s foil wallpaper that will probably be coming down, but it turns out this room is also not quite the time capsule it appears to be. Again, the model home photos provided the details the couple needed.

Previous owners had added faux–French country moldings to the vanity and its Zolatone finish had been painted. (Zolatone is a speckled, multicolor paint first used in Airstream trailers and car trunk interiors.) The planetary-looking balls had been removed from the divider and its brass rods covered with painted wooden turnings.

"The icing on the cake were the flower lamps," Johnney says sardonically. "They took cool atomic lights out and put in molded plastic flower-shaped lamps. For some reason, that picture of the original bath was the one I liked the most, and I wanted to make our bathroom exactly like that again."

"When we took down the wood dowels and found the brass underneath, you could see it was shinier where the cork balls had been," Jennie recalls.

"I'm the kind of guy who just goes along and occasionally something will pop up that I fixate on until it's done. I was like a pit bull—I was not going to let it go," Johnney laughs. "I could find 1" and 1 1/2" cork balls but I couldn't find 2".

▲▶ **PERIOD FIXTURES** like the corner tub and chrome towel rods that telescope into the wall would be nearly impossible to replace. The pink Kenmore space heater was an eBay find.

▶ **THE BED AND DRESSER** in the guest bedroom are from the Heywood-Wakefield Encore suite, while the nightstand is from the Trophy line. The fiberglass chair was made by Krueger Metal Products. Still one of the rooms with bold wall-to-wall from the previous owners, a neutral carpet, cork, or hardwood would be appropriate replacements. If you find a cool vintage lamp base, custom shades like these can be ordered from Moon Shine Lamp and Shade.

I had to order them from some place in Canada; I think they're fishing floats."

Jennie takes up the story: "We found one identical light fixture made by Lightolier, but weren't able to find a second. So we bought the next closest pair we could find on eBay and are saving the single in case we get lucky later."

A major lesson from this home is that original elements might be treasured by the next owner, so storing small items like light fixtures and hardware, or documenting the as-built condition in photos is the thoughtful thing to do. And when you do install new finishes in a midcentury ranch, sticking with the same style almost always works better than trend-driven choices—think of the Halls' new VCT floor versus wood-look laminates or faux-Tuscan ceramic tile.

Johnney and Jennie each have a parting nugget of advice for would-be homeowners. "If the house is built on a slab and still has the original plumbing, think twice," Johnney cautions. "We were lucky that they'd redone the plumbing here and ran it through the attic."

"Do what you like and take your time finding the right things" is Jennie's counsel on interiors. "And don't worry about what other people tell you if they're not into midcentury."

Original elements might be treasured by the next owner, so storing small items or documenting the as-built condition in photos is the thoughtful thing to do.

The home's exterior is a combination of traditional and midcentury zing—the beige man-made stone facade, shake-look roof, and aluminum windows get a kick from **the red, center-knob front door** and the wrought-iron porch supports.

▲ **WISELY, THE HALLS** picked up the red accent color on the garage door without going overboard.

L-SHAPED TRACT HOUSE, 1964
Calistoga, California
1,900 square feet
3 bedrooms, 2 baths

CRANK UP
THE VOLUME

In a neighborhood of nice but modest homes, the owner of this ranch house chose low-key elements like decomposed granite to replace a thirsty lawn.

◀ **OVERLEAF:** The space is assertively geometric, but has leavening curves and soft surfaces—the Ekornes lounge chair and ottoman, the couch pillows, and even the shag rug—to make it welcoming. The slat-topped table from Williams-Sonoma is teak, as are the vintage nesting tables near the fireplace. Under-cabinet fluorescents are recessed into the top of the orange volume; the large painting on the upper wall is by Toni Doilney.

▶ **WHITE IS THE PREDOMINANT COLOR** in the living and dining room, with a black sectional from Living Divani and inexpensive IKEA bookshelves grounding the neutral carpet. The black fireplace surround and built-in cabinets pick that up, while the orange section of wall plays nice with the vintage dining set and the new wood windows and doors.

THERE IS NOTHING MORE UBIQUITOUS THAN A RANCH WITH A TWO-CAR GARAGE DOMINATING the front facade—sometimes they're even mocked as "garage, with attached house." They line the streets of postwar developments across the nation, and it's still a favorite of developers looking to squeeze the most home onto a narrow lot. People decry these houses as shrines to the automobile and complain that they're ugly and their front doors are hard to find. What to do if this describes your ranch, and you're an architect like Pam Kinzie?

"The style was my one reservation when I bought this house," Pam admits. "I couldn't believe I was buying a 'snout house.' But now I think they have great potential; there are masses of suburbs with these homes."

Pam's issues with the house ranged from its hidden front door, small entry hall, and direct access from the garage blocked by a powder room, to awkward public rooms and an isolated kitchen. Yet because of her budget, local building ordinances, and the desire for neighborhood consistency, she didn't want to add a second story or expand the footprint. Done in spurts over a period of nine years, her remodel was both modest and extensive.

After buying in 2000, she painted the interior, added AC, and relocated the furnace into a spare bedroom closet. Once she realized she'd be staying put, Pam, in her 50s and the principal at Kinzie & Associates, began taking down minor walls, knowing a major reworking of the space was coming up. By 2007 she was ready.

An architect approaches a project from the perspective of function and problem solving long before style and aesthetics kick in. Foremost on her list was opening up the interior, which she accomplished by removing load-bearing walls and adding a hidden support beam in the main living area. Now, as you step into the ample foyer, you face a living/dining room with two lofty ceiling planes—one over the dining table that reflects the original roofline, and an even taller one over the seating area.

"I was initially going to open up the ceiling to the rafters, but when my structural engineer took a look, he told me we were going to have to reframe the portion of the back roof over the porch—he didn't feel it would be strong enough once we removed the bearing wall," Pam explains. "By extending the roofline [beyond the peak], we had room for a whole row of clerestories; it made such a difference in the space."

Pam changed out all of the existing vinyl windows to dual-glazed, metal-frame Milgard units and put in stacking Simpson-brand French doors leading to the covered porch. She even rebuilt a defunct corner fireplace in a more central location. Looking at the before floor plan (page 109), it's hard to imagine this room chopped up into discrete spaces.

The 21' x 18' living/dining area has an edited number of furnishings: a black sectional backed by bookcases, a vintage dining set, a melamine storage chest, a lounge chair and ottoman, and some side tables; not a coffee table or floor lamp in sight. Instead, the room is lit by three banks of windows and the overhead clerestories, and at night by fluorescents that wash the orange wall with light.

"Typically that's all I have turned on in the room in the evening," Pam says about the wall washers. "I do have a small floor lamp next to my cream-colored leather chair that I use sometimes for reading."

One of the challenges of a to-the-studs room remodel or new construction is anticipating where electrical plugs and light fixtures need to go in an environment you've yet to live in. "I wired for two additional lighting locations: a floor plug that is still coiled up under the house that I waited to install until I figured out how I was most likely going to arrange the sofa pieces; and a cable light system from the upper fireplace wall to the wall above the entry ceiling, passing over the dining room table. I'll put the cable system in at some point."

Just inside the front door, a curved, freestanding wall partially wraps the kitchen and points visitors toward the living room while it screens the view of the cooking area from the dining room. Because it's curved and doesn't reach to the ceiling, the dining area visually extends into the entry, keeping both from feeling cramped.

▲▶ **THE BUILT-IN CUPBOARD** to the right of the Majestic fireplace can be used for closed storage, or one or more of the doors removed to house a small or large television and other media. The Danish mid-century chair was designed by Kai Christensen, and the print is by Josh Hagler.

◀ **A BEAUTIFUL VIGNETTE** with purple accents playing off the warm oranges of the wall and furniture: the Danish-made dining table is midcentury, but the reupholstered chairs from Singapore are more recent. The cherry melamine buffet chest displays Balinese puppets, a watercolor by Taman VanScoy, a ceramic bowl by Matiwe oe Auzaila, and a spiral metal sculpture.

BATHING BEAUTIES

THE BATHS IN THIS BOOK REPRESENT A WHOLE RANGE OF AESTHETICS AND APPROACHES, from the Halls' and the Rissovers' virtually original rooms to decidedly contemporary choices. As with kitchen remodels, the best approach is to use materials that won't date your project in 10 years, and to craft a bath that's at home in a ranch house, not a spa or luxury hotel.

Many of the same counter and flooring materials that are appropriate to a midcentury kitchen have a place in baths, so "Vintage Kitchens" on page 90 is a good start. For other bathroom-specific items, here are some things to consider:

Fixtures Think classics, not fads: low, simple toilets, wall-hung or chrome-rimmed sinks, and standard tubs. Kohler's San Raphael toilet or Tahoe sink are nice, basic models, and while you can't go wrong with white, both of these styles are available in midcentury colors like yellow, blue, and gray. Duravit's Vero washbasin is another option; it's a modern take on the Halls' pink '50s sink. And while most vessel sinks will date stamp your room, Kohler's Vox Vessel is unfussy and sculptural.

Claw-foot or modern stand-alone vessel tubs aren't the right look, but some midcentury homes did have sunken Roman tubs that are similar to today's popular mosaic tile showers. American Standard's Spectra tub would look good in a modern or retro bath and, if you inherit an original cast-iron tub that's worn or the wrong color, a refinishing company can make it look new again—a paint process that will last about 10 years. If you're tempted by vintage fixtures at the local salvage yard, know that finding a faucet to fit or tank mechanisms may be difficult, and local codes may dictate low-flow toilets be in place when a home sells.

Tile Four-inch square field tile, like those on pages 49, 95, and 159 may not make your heart flutter, but they are almost indestructible, inexpensive, and were in use from the 1920s on. They're available at most home improvement stores. For some punchy colors, try Florida Tile's Tranquil line. Glass tile is a current darling, but it comes with installation challenges and is a trend that may become dated. One-inch or two-inch glazed ceramic or porcelain tile gives a similar look, and both are authentic midcentury materials; Appiani and Anthologia from Nemo Tile, or Daltile's color body porcelain Keystone line are some to look for. And subway tile sure is popular, but it was really designed for bungalow-era homes—if authenticity is important to you.

Kohler's Vox Vessel rectangular sink.

San Raphael toilet by Kohler.

One of Nemo Tile's Appiani Mix mosaics.

The before and after plans show how rethinking the spaces opened up the house while still keeping it in the original footprint.

Master Bedroom · **Closet** · **Bath** · **Bedroom** · **Laundry** · **Porch** · **Kitchen** · **Dining** · **Bedroom** · **Entry** · **Bath** · **Living Room** · **Garage**

NORTH

ORIGINAL PLAN

Master Bedroom · **Bath** · **Closet** · **Bedroom** · **Porch** · **Bath** · **Laundry** · **Kitchen** · **Living/Dining Room** · **Bedroom** · **Entry** · **Garage**

NORTH

NEW PLAN

▶ THE EGGPLANT-COLORED POST
supports a new beam that
spans the living/dining/
kitchen space, and the
glazed front door admits
much more light than its
predecessor. The liberal use
of art throughout the house
extends even to walls far
above head height. "You need
to inhabit the full volume, so
I extended the furnishings up
into that space," homeowner
Pam Kinzie says.

"I wanted to keep the ceiling low over the entry/
kitchen area, and have a higher ridge over the din-
ing/living space but still capture the light that was
coming in the clerestories," Pam explains. She cut
a large square opening into the kitchen ceiling so
that the light could enter, but it still has an intimate
feel. That floating ceiling houses incandescent Kona
pendants and fluorescent can lights because the
building code requires an equal number of the two
types of lighting.

Since the kitchen is on view, Pam addressed that
with some clever details. "Because the kitchen is
part of an open space, I wanted it to look as little
like a kitchen as possible," she says. Grain-matched
cherry plywood was used for new lower cabinets, so
it appears more like a volume—a favorite descrip-
tive word of Pam's that architects use to describe a
specific mass, such as a wall, roof, or in this case,
the block of cabinetry facing the living room.

As you step into the ample foyer, you face a living/dining room with two lofty ceiling planes creating a dramatic effect of structure and light.

"On the back wall, I used tongue-and-groove cedar siding for a horizontal line. The cabinet-maker planed down the material from ¾" to about ⅜" and mounted it on plywood to avoid cupping. This is intentionally different than the other cabinets so it looks more like wainscoting or a separate furniture piece—less of a kitchen look," she explains. "Those cabinets are only 12" deep so you're not reaching for things in the back, and the uppers are more accessible because you're not stretching over a deep lower cabinet. And I wanted the appliances to show as little as possible: the stove is a Jenn-Air downdraft, so there's no hood, and the refrigerator is tucked at the back and you only see an edge from the living room."

Although the cabinetry on that back wall was custom-made for the space, Pam reused the existing boxes on the peninsula cupboards, as well as some drawer faces that had a sculptural profile she liked. No ripping out for the sake of ripping out. She chose polished granite for the counters, the same material as the fireplace surround in the living room.

◄ **REUSING THE EXISTING CABINET BOXES** saved money and kept a still-sound material out of the landfill. Cabinetmaker Glenn Pope fabricated new cherry fronts and incorporated the previous sculptural top drawers into the design. A clever wine storage unit was made from leftover sections of the support beam pipe welded together, painted black, and cushioned with vinyl drawer liner.

► **PAM PLANNED** to extend the cedar wainscoting down the hall and into the master bedroom, but transitions at doorways proved too problematic. As it was, the installation required both a cabinetmaker and a finish carpenter to continue the material along the wall opposite the refrigerator. A fabric panel recessed into the wood covers an electrical panel, and the mitered corners of the doors show an architect's quest for precision.

Because the kitchen is part of an open space,
   I wanted it to look as little like a kitchen as possible.

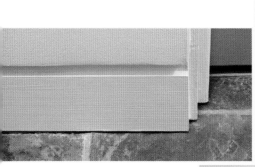

◄ SIMPLE ISN'T EASIER: in addition to refinishing the hollow-core interior doors with three coats of enamel and installing Valli&Valli lever hardware, Pam took the drywall back 6" around the doorways, cut the doorframes down so they were the same depth as the studs, and reinstalled wallboard over the frame with a crisp metal edge. Same with the baseboard: the drywall ends a little shy of the base and there's a metal J bead at the bottom that gives a much more modern look than applied molding. "That's just my architectural preference to have this really clean line—it's a lot of work that most people probably wouldn't think of," Pam concedes.

▶ THE RELOCATED HALLWAY BATH has an operable skylight in the slate shower and glass tile on its floor and the vanity top. Pam had her installer cut 3"-wide slate pieces out of 12" square stock, a similar technique to the floors in the chapter "Work of Art." Instead of a ubiquitous glass door, she uses a simple shower curtain for a more spacious feel in the smallish bath. The vanity holding the nickel-finished, hammered copper sink is a modified Madison credenza from Crate & Barrel. The wall-to-wall mirror amplifies the sense of space and takes the top of the window as its datum.

Like other homes in this book, Pam kept her color palette restrained and repeated materials. Slate tile begins on the front walk, continues into the entry and kitchen, then runs down the hall into the new baths. The pattern of the slatted kitchen cabinetry is echoed in the kerf cuts on the doors of the built-in storage by the fireplace. And the exterior paint color is also used on the tall wall in the kitchen and on the interior doors in the private areas.

"I looked at the house as one continuous whole for the palette, rather than room by room," she says. "Outside, it's a dull gray-green, quiet; but because it's a snout house, I needed to call attention to the door—the red draws your eye. Inside, it's white except for a few colored volumes that have to do with the architecture: the curved gold wall, the orange horizontal fireplace wall, the tall green volume in the kitchen, which you experience as background."

In addition to some other refinements—hallway skylights and new hardware, paint, and framing treatment for the existing hollow-core interior doors—the other major change was reworking a large laundry room to accommodate a master bedroom closet and the relocated second bath. Both bathrooms use slate on the floors, walls, and in the shower. They also share many of the same fixture choices, from Toto toilets to Kohler faucets and Restoration Hardware towel bars.

With a background in interiors, architecture, and project management, Pam was able to tweak her snout house so it's now more silk purse than sow's ear. And as both client and designer on this project, she's in a good position to give advice to others about working with a pro.

"The thing that's most helpful is if homeowners talk about what the problems are: how they live, what's working or not working for them. If they talk about the solution, I may not understand what's driving them to that," she says. "And if I understand, I might have some other options."

"People will have ideas they've seen in a magazine or at a friend's house or on TV, and they'll say, 'I want to do this here.' That is not as helpful as knowing why they want to do it, and sometimes the idea is something foreign to the house that they have." One last thing: "Discuss what is a comfortable budget range—that will play into what kinds of options might be considered. If you don't talk about money, you may waste a lot of time having a designer or contractor work on a plan that's not in an affordable range."

One cost-cutting idea from Pam's remodel is the bifold door system she devised from Simpson doors and her favorite hardware manufacturer, Häfele. A similar packaged system would have run significantly more, and both the doors and the hardware she chose

▶ **BY ELIMINATING** one of the doors into the master bath, Pam gained more usable square footage. "I didn't want the two baths exactly alike, but to have an underlying common approach and materials," she explains. Her cabinetmaker crafted a dark-stained maple vanity for this room, with a Kohler under-mount sink in the Absolute Black granite top, the same material she used in the kitchen and around the living room fireplace.

Both bathrooms use slate throughout and share many of the same fixture choices, from the toilets to the faucets and towel bars.

had unadorned, contemporary profiles. With this change, her home literally opens up to embrace its site, and the usable entertaining space doubles.

An example of one-thing-leads-to-another was the house/garage access issue that helped drive the remodel in the first place. Once the bathroom was relocated and the steps in the garage were built, the cars needed to shift to the left to pull in all the way and allow the door to close. The garage door placement had been subtly bugging her anyway, as it wasn't centered, so she committed to moving it. She looked extensively to find a simple door similar to the battered original she'd inherited, and finally discovered a sectional steel commercial door from Wayne-Dalton. But it turns out the new door needed to go as far to the left as possible. "And of course that meant I had to move the driveway too," Pam laughs ruefully. "That was one of those costs without much direct benefit."

"Experientially, the house feels much, much larger than it did before. This type of remodel is not as hard on the environment in terms of the use of resources, and it keeps the house in character with the neighborhood by not building out too large," she says.

"I've also worked on Eichler-type homes, which are much more flexible because of the post-and-beam construction. These snout houses are less flexible with

▸ **PAM CONFESSES** that the gas fireplace is more sterile than she imagined and isn't a feature she'd choose again. The bed, nightstands, and blue chair are from Scandinavian Designs, and the wool rug is by Kaleen. Art includes works by Charley Harper above the fireplace, John Johnson in the hallway, and over the bed, left to right, landscapes by Chris Newhard, Gil Amavisca, and Ginny Wing.

The
master
bedroom
gained a
walk-in
closet, an
in-wall
fireplace,
and
refinished
hardwood
floors.

▲ **FROM THE SLATE PATHWAY** to the red front door and the additional glazing, Pam's home is contemporary, yet homey.

▶ **THE BLACK PAINTED SIMPSON DOORS** and the metal storage unit (large enough to hold folding chairs) continue the color scheme out onto the covered porch. Teak is used again, too, this time in slatted Adirondack chairs.

their load-bearing walls, and they don't necessarily have a nice, clear architectural organization, but they have an intimate scale, they're usually one story, and there's a great opportunity for an indoor/outdoor connection.

"Ranches present a lot of opportunities, particularly if you have a contemporary orientation," Pam concludes. "Opening things up a little spatially and bringing more light in, no matter what you do stylistically, can really help make it more appropriate for today's living. You should respect the character that is there; it's not a bad character if you just pick the strong points and work with that."

MODERNIST TRACT HOUSE, 1958
San Mateo, California
2,010 square feet
3 bedrooms, 3 baths

ON TRACT

An Eichler home presents an almost blank street facade, but there's glass and architectural alchemy once you're in the private backyard.

◀ **OVERLEAF:** Although completely contemporary, the kitchen shares traits with the original Eichler design that preceded it—the suspended "flying coffin" cabinet, the modest galley footprint, and the sliding cupboard doors. Stripping a painted ceiling is an expensive and laborious job, so architect Mark Marcinik's crew concentrated on the Doug fir beams. The Olav fixtures are from Tango Lighting, and the painting on the blue wall is vintage.

▶ **MARK MARCINIK** gave the "hybrid plug-in" 10' ceilings, two feet higher than in the main house. "This house has a lot of glass but only 8' ceilings. Typically, Eichlers were built with 10' living areas and 8' in the bedroom wings. Ten feet allows you to do clerestories from the 8' height up," he explains. The yellow CB2 chairs tie in with the original front door, now used as a gate in the plasma-cut steel fence by Mark Bourne of Windsmith Design. The landscape is by Ric Lopez of Modernpast.

THE HOUSES OF CALIFORNIA BUILDER JOSEPH EICHLER HAVE A CULT FOLLOWING AMONG midcentury architecture fans. Their post-and-beam construction—which allows for huge expanses of glass and a wide-open layout—and unabashedly modern facades epitomize the look that people think of as "atomic" ranches. But they have some downsides too.

The bedrooms and baths are quite small, the radiant heating systems in the concrete slabs are often springing leaks by now, and deferred maintenance can be particularly rough on a house with a flat roof and thin plywood siding. Plus, with all that glass and minimal insulation, their energy usage can make for breathtaking utility bills. Javier Szwarcberg and Erica Smulever's home in the Eichler Highlands tract was just such an example—but not when they bought it.

Architect Mark Marcinik of the San Francisco firm M110 Architecture had worked with the previous owner on a whole-house renovation beginning in 2000. During the first phase, a new roof with an insulation barrier was put on, asbestos floor tile was replaced with slate, the interior beams were stripped, and most other surfaces painted. A few years later, a modern kitchen and fresh finishes in the dining room

▶ **FACING:** In the master bedroom addition, the steel roof and beams rest on cast-in-place concrete walls, and the floor is a slate-covered radiant-heated slab. The uncovered windows and skylight over the Modernica Fastback bed took some getting used to, but the owners now love to stargaze while in bed. The Eames LCW is from Herman Miller and generic Danish Modern slatted benches are used as nightstands; the matching lamps are Lighthouse by Pablo.

were tackled. By the time Erica and Javier toured the home in 2008, a master bedroom wing had been added, a feature the architect dubs a "plug-in hybrid."

"The idea was we wouldn't mess with the house too much, we'd just basically plug in a steel module at the back," Mark says. "The house then became a hybrid of steel and wood."

His love of Frank Lloyd Wright's work and Eichler's experimental X-100 steel-framed house, which is in the same San Mateo tract, heavily influenced the new master suite. "I worship the X-100—it's as good as anything Mies van der Rohe did. Prefab grips the imagination like Marxism: no matter how many times Marxism fails, people still believe in the concept," he exclaims. "And I love steel; it's something like Frank Lloyd Wright's concept of dry construction—you can bolt it together and move in without needing to plaster and paint. But of course that's a fantasy."

Frank Lloyd Wright's work and Joseph Eichler's experimental X-100 steel-framed house heavily influenced the new master suite.

▼ **A FRAMELESS CORNER WINDOW** opens up the view to the backyard, while a low operable window is one of several in the room that help vent excess heat and moisture. The purple bed linens seem to be a departure from the neutrals and the Frank Lloyd Wright Cherokee Red–colored steel, but two concrete walls are upholstered with similar-colored fabric, one at the foot of the bed and the other off camera to the right. Behind the headboard wall is a soaking tub, and the quilt is by Denyse Schmidt. The Paul McCobb dresser is vintage, as are the green bullet lamp and the Italian glass platter.

▲ **AIR BUBBLES,** snap-tie dimples, and the pattern of the forms show on the concrete wall by the Duravit tub. Homeowners Javier Szwarcberg and Erica Smulever say there are two downsides to the dual-purpose room: it takes longer to heat, and a sleeping partner can be disturbed by the shower (so the first one up tends to use one of the other baths).

A look inside the 760-square-foot room shows its X-100 similarities: the corrugated steel ceiling, orange-painted posts and beams, and expansive glass that contrasts with cast-in-place concrete walls. The vibe is more industrial modernist than the home's original bedrooms and baths, what with its stripped-down hard surfaces, but wood and textiles help warm it up, just as we've seen in earlier chapters.

Mark wanted the bedroom and bath to be one integrated space. A tub for two is on the other side of the headboard wall, while the shower, toilet room, and closets line an exterior wall facing the side yard. One long wall-hung cabinet functions as both a vanity in the bath and a dresser in the bedroom. On the window wall, the material changes from insulated glass, which helps with condensation issues, to mirrored glass over the sinks.

"The addition is structure and finish at the same time," Mark says. "The tightness that I like in architecture is when it's not three layers: a fake layer for beauty, a structural layer, and a layer for waterproofing or something like that. What you see here is what you get; everything is exposed."

The master suite was a huge selling point to Erica and Javier, but their love of midcentury drew them to the neighborhood and the original house as well. Javier, 40, a physician, and Erica, 39, a psychologist and social worker who's on career hiatus to raise their two children, grew up in custom homes in Peru and Argentina. Wood, slate, brick, extensive windows, and a strong inside/outside connection were familiar themes.

"I fell in love with modern architecture after reading a few issues of *Arts & Architecture* that my parents had, over and over; as a matter of fact, I wanted to be an architect," says Javier. "Growing up in those homes took some of the fear factor away about living in a house that's not the norm. We're more willing to experiment and try things that are new."

This Eichler's biggest flaw, in Mark's view, was the transparency of the public rooms facing the street. Believed to be a model home for the tract, the glass walls put residents on display to passing traffic. His first proposal to the previous owner was to erect a privacy fence, but that didn't happen until 2009, when Erica and Javier had obscure glass and Cor-Ten steel panels installed. This provided them with a front court-yard and allowed their two children the freedom to run throughout the yard.

During the master suite addition, the wall between the living room and an original bedroom came down to give access to the new space. This created a long, narrow living room that the previous owner later

Eichler's post-and-beam construction and unabashedly modern facades epitomize the look that people think of as "atomic" ranches.

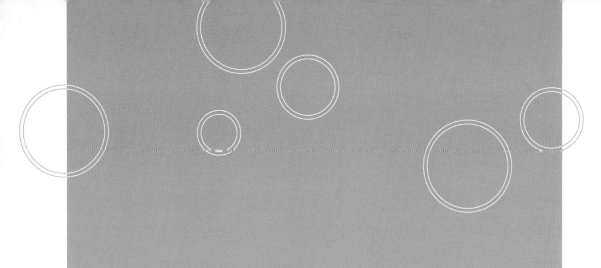

ARCHITECTURAL
WINDOWS

MANY HOMEOWNERS ARE INTERESTED IN REPLACING ORIGINAL WINDOWS, with the thought that new units will halve their utility bills and pay for themselves. Window manufacturers are only too happy to facilitate that mind-set. But it's an expensive proposition that can alter the look of your midcentury house, damage siding and interior wall surfaces, and lead to issues with failed window seals down the road. You should know about the pros and cons going in.

"Every time I do the cost efficiency on changing out windows, it doesn't make any sense," says San Francisco architect Mark Marcinik. "If you have a 10' high and 6' wide window that's single pane, and you're contemplating changing it out, you'll never get your money back in energy savings. And insulated glass doesn't necessarily create energy savings—it depends on how you use it."

Your climate will dictate if heat loss or gain will be your primary focus, but other concerns may come into play as well, such as condensation and fading of textiles or flooring. Research the features of low-e and double-pane units with a knowledgeable pro, preferably someone who can understand your house will require something beyond the norm. Any way you slice it, the R-factor of a glass wall will be in the R-1 to R-4 range, as opposed to R-11 to R-28 for a well-insulated wall.

Then there are the aesthetics. "I love the thin profile of the windows in the living room and dining room of my ranch in Portland," says architect Mark Engberg. "The windows would look significantly different if they were replaced—clunkier, with less glass."

Pam Kinzie's home came to her with vinyl windows in place; her architect's sensibilities dictated a change. "Natural materials seem appropriate to ranch homes, and I have a personal hesitancy about plastic," she says. "I went back to dual-glazed metal, though you could argue the energy efficiency of the metal frames."

If new windows *are* on the to-do list, wood or metal frames are period-appropriate; vinyl cladding is not. For large fixed panes, look at commercial "storefront-style" windows or IGUs (insulated glass units) if your windows aren't square or were oddball custom sizes when the home was built. If you have a home with sliding glass doors or other types of aluminum windows, such as awning, casement, or horizontal sliders, Arcadia, Blomberg, Milgard, Marlin, and Peerless are brands to consider. And both replacement parts and new models of louver (aka jalousie) windows, which offer great airflow, are available from Tafco Corporation and Pickens Window Service. If your ranch is more traditional and has double-hung wood windows, a local sash and door company can usually offer wood frame replacements.

Aluminum-frame sliding glass doors from Blomberg Window Systems in the atrium of another Eichler home.

Installing obscure glass and Cor-Ten steel panels provided a front courtyard, allowing privacy from the street.

Master Bedroom

Patio

Family Room

Bath

Living Room

D | W

Bath

Dining Room

Bedroom

Bedroom

Kitchen

Garage

▼ **LOOKING TOWARD** the new wing from the living room, the door to the patio is near the vintage green Eames Aluminum Group chair, and behind the midcentury shelving unit is the family room. The frosted glass window funnels more light into the family room while maintaining privacy when it's used as a guest room.

considered dividing with a folding door. Once they were living there, Javier and Erica felt that a dedicated den/guest room for extended visits from their families was a higher priority than the large living room.

The couple clicked with Mark and thought it would be smart to continue with the same architect for any additional projects. "The '80s great room is pretty much dead—the TV or a video game can just take over 1,000 square feet," the architect says. "This is more like a den concept where you can close the door and have privacy; today, a media room is also typically a guest bedroom." To that end, a stainless steel–clad wall with vintage shelving units now separates the two functions.

The living room, like some others we've seen in previous chapters, was the most vexing space, and it's still a work in progress. "The shape of the living room and the position of the fireplace make it hard," Erica comments. "We put the couch on the green wall, but that didn't work."

▶ **THIS VIEW OF THE LIVING ROOM** shows the constraints to furniture arrangement. The location of the fireplace argues for a couch, a chair, and a small coffee table, yet they need access to storage units installed behind the Le Corbusier LC2 sofa. Against the green Venetian plaster wall is a Danish Modern bench, an unattributed floor lamp, and a vintage fiberglass rocker. The Alexander Calder serigraph, the wall clock, and the red cotton rugs are also midcentury, while the white coffee table is from Design Within Reach.

"You can't put furniture in front of the glass walls. The house is about bringing the outside in."

▲ **THE GLASS DOORS** and light scale of the upper cabinetry keep it from dominating the room and blocking the view to the rest of the house; note the unobtrusive Gaggenau exhaust fan built into the bottom of the cabinet. Metal elements include ventilated aluminum supports under the shelf behind the cooktop and the cantilevered 1¼"-thick slate counter, and the cladding on the 4" x 4" posts near the adjunct storage units.

▲ **ON THE SINK WALL,**
the oven and dishwasher are
Gaggenau, and the fridge is
an Amana. The stainless steel
cabinetry includes a hidden
spice compartment with a rustic
birch handle and a pullout towel
bar, and the blue cabinet door
up top is dichroic glass.

"You have to get away from the notion of symmetry," Javier adds. "And you can't put furniture in front of the glass walls," Erica continues. "The house is about bringing the outside in."

"We were going to move the strangely situated fireplace over by one window bay," Mark says, "but things like that are not high-value when it comes to an appraisal." Instead, the room is in effect a compact inglenook around the hearth with a circulation hub that leads to the kitchen, the patio, the master bedroom, the family room, and on the far side of the yellow accent wall, down the hall to the kids' wing or to the front door.

Sharing the living room volume is the kitchen/dining area. In the previous renovation, the homeowner milled solid Douglas fir in the style of Eichler grooved siding for the dining room wall, and a custom wenge wood credenza was hung on it. According to the original floor plan, the current dining space was intended as a family room; the '50s family was to eat at a swiveling five-foot table connected to the kitchen island. Today, Javier and Erica have two resin-topped dining tables that can be pushed together for company, but as often as not, the family grabs their meals at the cantilevered slate kitchen counter.

The stainless steel kitchen also has wenge wood cabinets with sliding upper doors of mixed materials: ribbed glass, concrete board, and dichroic glass. Most items are put away to keep the counters clear, but a since-discontinued stainless steel storage system by Boom holds necessities on the backsplash. For all of its high-tech Euro look, Erica reports the kitchen works just great for a family,

▲▶ **THE DOUGLAS FIR BEAMS** and wall paneling, the wenge wood cabinetry and credenza, and the slate counter and floor show the power of repeating elements within a room. Illumination includes up lights, a Nelson bubble lamp over the dining table, and a larger version of the Lighthouse prism lamps in the master bedroom. The vintage Saarinen chairs are a blue similar to the accent wall in the kitchen.

In the previous renovation, the home-owner milled solid Douglas fir in the style of Eichler grooved siding for the dining room wall, and a custom credenza was hung on it.

though they did put in additional storage units between the kitchen and living room, and she keeps bigger items like the pasta maker and paella pan in the garage.

Two other recent projects included a cosmetic upgrade to the kids' bath and converting a walk-in closet next to the family room into an office. In the latter, Mark added a glass door leading to the side yard, which solved the problem of toys and bikes cluttering the slate patio off the living room. Now the children can ride on the hardscape and their playthings are corralled in a part of the yard with minimal views from the house.

Although the remodel doesn't look like it was done on a budget, Mark points out that many of the materials were affordable or bought secondhand. The previous owner found a cheap source for the solid wenge wood used in the kitchen and, instead of concrete counters that cost $1,000 per linear foot, the master suite used Cembonit cement board, which at the time of construction ran about $100 a sheet. In the later kids' bath upgrade, they substituted HardieBacker board at $10 a sheet on the walls, as the Cembonit had grown too pricey.

Affordable anodized aluminum channeling appears as reveal trim and towel bars in the hallway bath, and as pulls on the cabinetry in the master bedroom. And the 3form laminated plastic used as an accent in the kids' bath and living room storage units was a craigslist remnant, as was a new wood and glass front door.

The house came with a rather unique feature: a backyard pad for travel trailers. "The first owner got aluminum fever from me," Mark jokes. "The idea was a man cave off the family room—an adult tree house. He had three little Airstreams at one point."

Javier also loved that concept and bought a 1976 31' Airstream from its 82-year-old original owner, who delivered it the day the family moved into the house. Unfortunately, it barely fit—we're talking 1½" clearances here—and was too big to tow on vacations. Now they have a 1952 Shasta, one of the vintage trailers nicknamed "canned hams."

◄ IN ARI AND
JULIETTE'S BATH,
an affordable remodel included
some of the same elements as
in the rest of the house—slate,
cement board, and aluminum.

Keeping the existing toilet and
tub, Mark Marcinik recom-
mended a wall-hung Duravit
Scola sink, which is available
with the basin on the left or
right, centered for a corner
installation, and with or without

chrome legs. The storage cabinet
and the metal Grundtal toilet
seat are both from IKEA, and the
Tango Olav light over the mirror
is mounted on 3form laminate,
which also wraps the cabinet.

**▲ THE KIDS' BATH
WALLS** were clad with
Hardie cement board, a
mold-resistant material that's
90 percent portland cement and
ground sand, finished with aluminum reveal panel trim from
Fry Reglet. Mark had the crew
sand and install the cement
board with the back side facing
out, and wider aluminum stock
is used as towel bars.

**◄ THE MASTER
BEDROOM VANITY**
is made from Douglas fir, the
same wood as the posts and
beams in the original portion
of the house. Cembonit stands
in for far more costly concrete
counters, which hold Duravit
vessel sinks and Grohe faucets.
The frosted glass door to
the right is the shower, and
reflected in the mirror are doors
to the commode and the closets.

The couple had been accumulating midcentury furnishings for about 10 years—some with a pedigree, others generic; some reissued, others from eBay. Initially, Erica's taste was more cutting-edge modern, while Javier favored a retro look; they found compromise with Danish Modern, teak, chrome, and leather. "I used to be pushier when I was younger, but this is our mutual living space, so we both have to be onboard," Javier says about their selection process.

The couple raves about the functionality of the vintage wall storage units they have all over the house, including a Drexel model in the family room. Taking up no floor space, they're great for display, storage, media, and working on a laptop. "The beauty of the wall units is that you can split them up according to the space you have," Erica says. They even found two matching units—one from a St. Louis vintage store for $1,000 and the

▲ IN SON ARI'S
ROOM, two midcentury
wall units can be used for
display, clothing, board
games, small toys, or school
supplies, and as a mini
computing center. The orange
storage units are Cubitec from
Design Within Reach, a shape
motif picked up in the area rug
and flooring.

▼ **THE STAINLESS STEEL WALL** clad with inexpensive IKEA panels continues the metal theme of the addition and the kitchen. The surface of the hallway on the right is similarly unique—grain-end wood blocks crafted by the previous owner.

▲ **THE FORMER MASTER BEDROOM** is now a den/guest room with a foldout couch from Design Within Reach and an adjoining bath behind the wall with the sunflowers. Vintage furnishings include a Paul McCobb dresser similar to that in the master bedroom, a Drexel wall unit, a Dove lamp from the '80s, and a Persian rug.

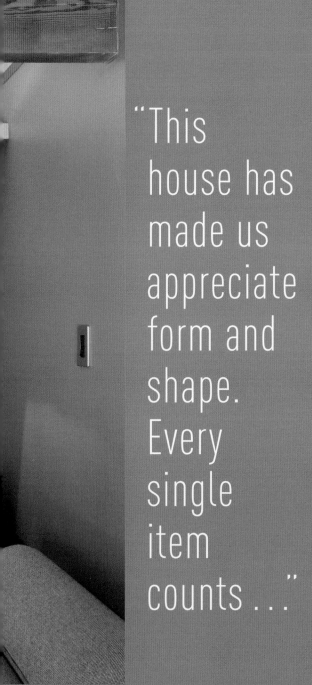

"This house has made us appreciate form and shape. Every single item counts ..."

▲ **THE BRIGHT YELLOW OFFICE,** formerly the bedroom closet and connector to the bath, has an Aeron task chair and the same wall unit as in Ari's room. The new windows and door open onto the Airstream dock where the kids play.

other at a New Jersey estate sale for $60—that are in the office and their son's room.

"Lots of neighbors remarked that these wall units were in place when they moved in and that they removed them and put them in their garages," Javier relates. "But now that they see how good and modern they are, they plan to dust them off and put them back up."

"This house has made us appreciate form and shape," Erica adds. "Every single item counts and you have to keep moving it until it's in the right spot. Before, we would see plates we liked and just buy them; now we say, That won't go with the house," she laughs. "It's changing and shaping us."

RAISED RANCH, 1953
Alexandria, Virginia
1,600 square feet
4 bedrooms, 3 baths

ARTISTS'
COLLECTIVE

Situated in a suburban forest, this modernist ranch has fewer direct indoor/outdoor connections than some, but the views and interior are amazing.

◀ OVERLEAF: The second story of this Hollin Hills home has a dramatic butterfly roofline and views akin to a tree house.

▶ THE BRICK FIREPLACE AND PANELING were already painted when Eric Margry and Linda Hesh bought the house. Their Heywood-Wakefield club chair, biomorphic sofa, and coffee table are all vintage, but the red chair and end table are affordable IKEA pieces. An L-shaped sectional and chrome and leather seating would have given the room a masculine feel; instead, the art, fabrics, and furniture profiles are more lighthearted. "Our colors in the living room play off each other but don't match; they're the same palette and they all have curves," Linda explains. Two works by Mequitta Ahuja hang over the IKEA display cabinets.

HOLLIN HILLS, A DEVELOPMENT LOCATED A FEW MILES OUTSIDE OF WASHINGTON, D.C., was built on 300 rolling, wooded acres between 1949 and 1971. Charles Goodman (the same architect responsible for the prefab Alcoa house in the chapter "Full Metal Jacket") designed 450 houses in nine basic models; each is sited to take advantage of its topography and minimize views of its neighbors. In a region of neoclassic homes, the neighborhood is a mecca for modern architecture fans.

One 1953 butterfly roof model—which looks like *The Incredibles* house set on a brick pedestal—belongs to Linda Hesh and Eric Margry, an idiosyncratic late-50s couple who like to get their hands dirty when it comes to home improvement. After losing several Hollin Hills homes in bidding wars, in 2003 the pair got lucky, finding one with a large studio addition at the rear. Its unusual floor plan starts with two front doors, a downstairs kitchen and dining room, and the living room and bedrooms up top.

After persevering through unsexy improvements like a new roof, heat pump, insulation, windows, and sewage line, the couple was able to tackle more creative projects. To start, the exterior was painted taupe, the front door orange, and the windows and interior walls gallery white.

"The one thing that Goodman wasn't good at was entryways," says Linda, a photography-based artist. "Our orange door opens directly to the staircase. We picked the door color to go with the brick and the sculpture next to the driveway." The eye-catching color also tells visitors which door to approach when arriving for the first time.

Once you climb the stairs, the living room announces that the homeowners are serious about art. Every wall and flat surface holds an original work by Linda or the numerous artist friends they've made in their 20-plus years together. Art glass, paintings, prints, sculptures, drawings, photographs, and crafts abound. Yet, the curated look of a gallery prevails.

In a niche at the top of the stairs is a cabinet thought to be an Alvar Aalto design, now stained red and black—it was the '80s, Linda says, and who knew better? It displays a substantial glass vessel by Anthony Corradetti, whose work is in the

Smithsonian. Nearby, a vintage Eames rocker is paired with a soda bottle sculpture by Dan Steinhilber, a D.C. artist whose materials include trash bags, gum, and packing peanuts.

"We totally believe that artists should buy art," Linda says. "For people who are not used to looking at art, go to museums, to galleries, look online and try to figure out what you like instead of immediately rushing out to buy something. Art can be so inexpensive; you can get something at a student show that's really fabulous for $200."

"You can start small, and when you realize how exciting it is to buy something you really like, you'll make an easier decision the next time," adds Eric, who is a jewelry designer and hand engraver. Their own purchases include everything from lowbrow thrift store prints to a mixed-media piece brought back from the Netherlands folded into a shopping bag. Their high-low approach applies to furnishings as well, an aesthetic Linda dubs "the sacred and the profane."

By the fireplace, a Marcel Wanders floor lamp with a drunken-looking shade—it gives some of their neighbors fits, they're told—arches over an Adrian Pearsall coffee table, and IKEA cabinets hold dozens of beautiful, funny, and disturbing objects. In the same area, a curved couch that Linda likes to think is by Vladimir Kagan is grouped with a Heywood-Wakefield Ladies' Club chair and a circular IKEA armchair. These homeowners have the confidence to combine dissimilar art pieces, price

▲ THE VIEW FROM THE FRONT DOOR shows a sliver of the downstairs multipurpose room before one takes the stairs up to the living room. A sleeper sofa from Dellarobbia covered in a vintage-look fabric is paired with one of four baby Bertoia chairs the couple bought at a yard sale, complete with original rubbery paint. The computer table is IKEA, and the orange street sign platter is by Boris Bally.

▼ **YOU'LL NOTICE THAT** area rugs don't anchor the furniture groupings, but instead the hardwood floors function as a neutral ground for the gallery-like art collection. Distinctive touches include the original upholstery on the Heywood-Wakefield chair; the Pearsall coffee table, which shares design elements with a Noguchi table, but is far less ubiquitous; and the abstract above the fireplace by Joe Cooper. At the far end of the living room, the carpeted area is the transition to the studio addition. The lounge chair and ottoman are by Plycraft.

▲ A MIXED-MEDIA HORSEHAIR PIECE by Dutch artist Marian Bijlenga hangs over the maybe-Aalto cabinet. To the right is the hallway leading to the bedrooms and the stairway from the entry; on the left, a curved 1981 addition connects an art gallery built in 1969 to the home. The '80s-style track lighting is a good way to illuminate a variety of artwork without tearing into walls and ceilings.

Linda painted and installed 123 pieces of white felt on the upstairs vertical blinds to give them depth, softness, and insulating properties.

points, and furniture styles, and that makes their house look like no other.

"We like to mix up contemporary design with vintage, hence the current Dutch tilting floor lamp and the IKEA PS white table—PS is their 'design' line," Linda explains. "Mid-century design was really a highlight of industrial design, when form and function matched. That's why so many contemporary designers look to midcentury modern.

"An Eames chair is ergonomically designed, as opposed to what you'd buy at Target today. It was relatively inexpensive and designed for the masses; there's a lot that's stripped away, and there's no excess padding to make it look comfortable when it's not. That's why we like '50s furniture: it's functional and appealing to the eye."

◀ DAN STEINHILBER'S BOTTLE SCULPTURE and a painting by Huck Snyder contribute to this corner vignette. The telescoping slat-top bench, a style made by many U.S. and European companies, holds a hairpin-leg table lamp given to them by a friend. "Hollin Hills yard sales are incredible, since the first homeowners bought a lot of now-iconic furniture in bulk," comments Linda. "The gray Eames rocker came from the house next door."

▶ A BEAUTIFUL,
QUIET CORNER
of the living room houses
a vintage Dux lounge
chair and ottoman and
a framed piece by Linda
called *I Want What We
Had*. The woven helmet
by Katharine Cobey on
the stand is elevated by
an artful stack of books,
which lifts it to a pleasing
height on the wall; small
objects like the ceramic
heads on the IKEA table
make you draw closer to
examine them.

"We totally believe that artists should buy art. You can start small, and when you realize how exciting it is to buy something you really like, you'll make an easier decision the next time."

◀ A WORD PIECE
over the '60s bar is by
Tim Palmer, and the
pencil point jute child's
chair was found at a
yard sale.

ask not for whom the bell tolls, it's toll free...

"But why is my house arranged in vignettes? Why do I do that?" she wonders aloud, when asked to analyze their design ethos. "The reason certain art looks good is because of its proportions, which all has to do with body proportions. To us, certain things look good next to each other or in a certain position. I get upset when the chair isn't put back in the same place after vacuuming. To me, it only looks right in this one place—but I know that's obsessive."

The living room has a layout that lends itself to Linda's vignette obsession: overlooking the staircase is a dead-end corner next to a tall window and, on the opposite end, a carpeted portion that's the connector to the 1,400-square-foot studio. They've turned the latter into a bar/lounge area and the former into a reading nook.

One notices that orange and red are recurring themes in the house—from the driveway sculpture to the front door to the pillow and art in a tableau just inside that door. Upstairs, furniture and various artwork pick up on the scheme, and a peek in the recently redone bath confirms their attraction to vibrant color.

EXTERIOR HUES

THE COLORS YOU SEE DRIVING THROUGH AN EICHLER NEIGHBORHOOD, or one with a historic preservationist bent like Arapahoe Acres near Denver, are taupes, muted greens, browns, and grays with lighter trim. They tend to have saturated accent colors on the front doors—pumpkin, gold, red, turquoise. And, as we've seen with several modernist homes in this book, the brick facades, window walls, and expanses of natural wood can mean that there are fewer areas to actually stain or paint.

"I've always been fascinated by ranch houses that are deep earth tones on the exterior—dark browns, dark green, charcoal," says Portland architect Mark Engberg. "To me they look better the darker they are. Inherently, ranches aren't sitting on the earth like a Craftsman—they seem more naturally integrated to the plain of the earth, almost like an extension of the Prairie style."

More traditional ranches like those in the chapters "Retro Gem" and "Crank Up the Volume" offer larger canvases for color. Clapboards, raked cedar shakes, board and batten, and variations on T-111 siding are some common exterior claddings, often in combination with stone or brick accent walls, chimneys, and planters. If your home has unpainted brick, look for paint colors that complement your particular variety; this can take some trial and error, which makes sample cans a good investment. Painting over brick may seem like a way to modernize your ranch, but it destroys an original material and will ratchet up your maintenance significantly in coming years as the paint naturally flakes off the masonry.

Some tips on midcentury architectural details: exposed beams should be painted the same color inside and out, and deep soffits (the underside of a roof overhang) can be a place for contrasts—an accent that matches the front door, perhaps, or a lighter version of your body color if your house is heavily shaded. And if you have a split-level, a darker shade on the bottom portion tends to look better than the reverse.

If you're a fan of "fun" colors, instead of painting your whole house peach with acid green accents, try the vibrant hue on something modest, such as shutters or a door, fence, or mailbox like on the house in the chapter "Retro Gem" (pages 100-01). And no Painted Lady Victorian schemes: three related earth-tone shades are a good rule of thumb. Dunn-Edwards has a Ranch color palette, and Benjamin Moore (excellent paint, by the way) offers various online tools, including a fan deck that, while not midcentury per se, gives those of us without an innate color sense a good starting point.

Earthy chocolate brown, with just enough white and charcoal accents to give it definition, grounds this 1964 Eichler home to its suburban yard.

The floor plans show a typical conformation of this model before the studio addition upstairs and ground-floor remodel.

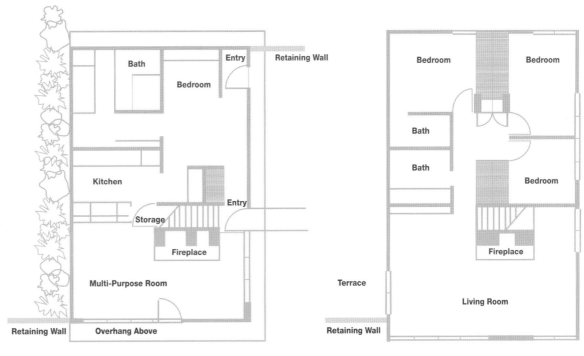

GROUND FLOOR PLAN

Retaining Wall
Entry
Bath
Bedroom
Kitchen
Entry
Storage
Fireplace
Multi-Purpose Room
Retaining Wall   Overhang Above

FIRST FLOOR PLAN

Bedroom
Bedroom
Bath
Bath
Bedroom
Terrace
Fireplace
Retaining Wall
Living Room

The bath is one of two on this level, and it combines original elements, vintage-look materials, and contemporary fixtures and finishes in a harmonious mix. This era of Hollin Hills bathrooms all had a long laminate vanity with one smallish sink and a wall-spanning mirror. They kept the cabinet, mirror, and sink, and installed a new laminate counter to match the orange rubber showerheads Linda had fallen for. When a large stall shower replaced the bathtub, that triggered tile-matching issues.

"Eric obsessively decided he wanted to keep the one wall of original tile, which meant we had to find something that would coordinate," Linda says. "That gray tile is all over Hollin Hills," Eric explains. "If we ripped it out we would have had to take the cabinet out and there's no way we would have gotten it back in. We switched out any cracked tiles, and it looks pretty good."

Matte glass tile in shades of gray, laboriously laid by Eric, looks similar to the one-inch ceramic mosaic used in postwar homes. But the creative couple is often somewhat dissatisfied with their options when facing a project such as this.

"We studied art history and all of its different periods," says Eric. "I'm originally from Holland, and when you go to a store there you have a much larger choice of well-designed products. Something as small as a nail brush would be available in different colors."

"And beautifully designed in a way that's inherent with how the product will work, as well as your pleasure while using it," interjects Linda.

"Design there is much more accentuated," Eric continues. "But it's getting better here. When I first moved to the U.S. in the '80s, every product was light blue or beige."

▲ THE AGAPE KAA
SHOWER FIXTURES
were the driving reason behind the accent color in the bath. No longer available, the rubber showerhead puffs up like a blowfish when the water flows. The glass mosaic tile is from Bella Tile in New York City, the stainless fixtures are Hansgrohe, and the clutter-busting dispensers are Blomus.

◄ **THIS VIEW** of the newly renovated bath shows the resurfaced cabinet and original long mirror and sink. When the addition to the house was built, the shorter mirror above the towel bar replaced a window. In a sort of homage, Eric added a window to the new shower that looks out to his plunger-cum-sculpture over the toilet. He also built sliding doors surfaced with aluminum-colored laminate for the vanity, the same material used on the boxed lighting element, which has dimmable down lights and a wall-washing fluorescent tube on top. "We do try to honor that we're in a '50s house," says Linda. "The counter is a basket-weave Formica pattern called Atomic Orange."

▼ THE DOWNSTAIRS MULTIPURPOSE ROOM has seating facing another fireplace and a dining area off the kitchen. The Italian table and chairs were purchased in Montreal, and the Milliken Oxygen commercial carpet has a pattern that looks like an old television screen. Drapes from Smith+Noble are hung from a hospital track on the ceiling, and the view of the new beam over the cooking area shows Eric's solution for incorporating a heavy-duty exhaust fan and stereo speakers into the structure. On the wall are two photographs by Linda.

Downstairs, they put in an IKEA kitchen when the original metal cabinetry turned out to be rusted, thanks to an unsoldered water pipe in the wall. They expanded the footprint into the dining room by 12" because they couldn't open opposing cabinets at the same time, and installed a Marmoleum floor. "Linoleum floors are almost everywhere in Holland," Eric says. "If you drop something, it doesn't break, and it's all natural, very comfortable, and it comes in very strange colors—perfect for us."

His biggest hurdle was replacing three support posts between the dining room and the kitchen with a beam, and incorporating a larger exhaust fan suitable for the Viking stove into that same area. Linda's creative contribution was the decorative panel on the front of the refrigerator—an oversize print of the pattern on their Franciscan Starburst dishes. Now the kitchen and dining room communicate freely, and the cook has a view unmarred by a bunch of bars.

In the bunker-like portion of the lower floor, down the hallway from the kitchen and den, was

▲ THE COUPLE had an IKEA kitchen previously and didn't hesitate to install one in this home. "Their kitchens are better made than some other IKEA products," Linda comments. "We asked ourselves, Do we want to spend $2,000 on counters or $90? But the laminate is starting to get messed up; there's a reason why it's $90." The green vintage casserole is always on display on the six-burner Viking stove; a fragmented landscape by Linda hangs nearby.

▶ THERE'S A MODEST AMOUNT of counter space flanking the Oliveri sink, but it works fine for the couple, who used power strips under the cabinetry instead of piercing the backsplash with outlets. The Amana fridge is clad with a starburst print protected by Plexiglas.

▼ **THE FRONT DOOR** with the narrow window (page 167) leads to the new guest suite. A bike-storage area to the right of the bed alcove is hidden behind a Smith+Noble shade, and the gray felt–covered bed pulls out on casters for sleeping and access to built-ins. In most Hollin Hills homes with the same floor plan, this area is purely storage.

a large, windowless black room that the previous owners used as a dining space and American Indian artifacts gallery. Eric and Linda took one look and thought it would make a great guest suite—the more womb-like the better.

A window and a door were unearthed behind Sheetrock, and when the couple was done rearranging partition walls, the area included a full bath, laundry area, sleeping alcove, bicycle storage, and writing desk. The headroom is low—from six to eight feet high—but semigloss, off-white paint makes the room very appealing and it becomes a magnet during parties, precisely because of its cozy, nesting qualities.

Texture plays a big part in the suite's success. A fluffy shag area rug, linen-like shades, and rough slate tiles around the bath are some of the elements. The couple made an unusual flooring choice—resin-coated pebbles more commonly used for pool decking—and it established a natural theme that's carried into the bath.

▲ **THE WALL-HUNG
DESK** (the leg is just for
fun) is Linda's joke on the
ubiquity of motel desks.
A drawer module from a
midcentury wall unit (like
those in the Eichler in the
chapter "On Tract") is narrow enough to not impinge
on the circulation pattern
from the doorway, and the
comically low Bertoia
chair makes it apparent
that this is a vignette,
not a desk designed for
work. The shade on the one
window in the room is the
same material as that on
the bicycle closet, and the
print of the vintage car is a
thrift store find.

◀ **A SMALL LAMP**
and Linda's photograph
of trees in a niche in the
storage wall substitutes for
a window. The three inex-
pensive framed and matted
pieces also came from a
secondhand store.

▼ **AN OPAQUE GLASS BARN DOOR** closes off the bathroom without requiring any room to swing. Reflected in the mirror is the laundry area behind the tree-print curtains, the same fabric used for the pillows on the bed. Another repeat is the pebble pattern of the flooring on the door fronts. The butterfly-shaped tub—a nod to the home's roof—is by Hoesch and the sink is from IKEA. Art includes the three ceramic wall sculptures by Laurel Lukaszewski and a thrift store portrait on the counter.

▸▴ **THE DOWNSTAIRS BATH** originally had five doors and was completely reworked by the couple. Eric built the wall-hung cabinets of birch plywood stained white. Alexandra Solmssen's photo picks up the colors of the slate wall by the tub.

"The guest bath was inspired by Richard Serra's huge rusted steel structures and how they contrast with white gallery walls," Linda explains. "We actually wanted to put rusted steel sprayed with lacquer on the wall next to the tub, but it was very expensive for two sheets that big. Instead, we used inexpensive slate you get at a home improvement store, which has the same roughness and coloration."

Eric did most of the construction in the guest suite, from building walls and hiding the heating ducts with intricate drywall sheathing to fabricating cabinets and a tub surround. "In several places he installed a light and a piece of textured Plexiglas that's sort of a skylight look with a larger field of light coming down," Linda points out.

"Since we're not architects, we'll lay tape on the floors or put up cardboard to figure out if layouts will work. This is an unusual L-shaped room, so we had to figure out how much space you really needed between a tub and a wall. It's a very low-tech way to do it because we didn't go to architecture school," she says.

In addition to sourcing all of the materials and fixtures, and collaborating with Eric on the design, Linda gave the vanity's sliding doors a distinctive artistic touch: a photo of the floor texture sandwiched between plastic, similar to the refrigerator door treatment. And that's not all.

"I do the fussy, obsessive stuff," she volunteers. "For the slate around the tub, I used a new type of grout that you combine with polymer and custom-mixed the color for each seam in the slate."

"I don't get involved in that," Eric says drily. "I have to figure out things like building the wall to accommodate the plumbing. Making jewelry and making furniture are similar: if you have the right equipment, it's not that difficult to make the parts and put them together."

The neighborhood was preparing a nomination to the National Trust for Historic Preservation when we visited, which seemed to be meeting with little homeowner resistance. "The design review committee already gives people plenty to debate," Linda observes wryly. "When Hollin Hills was built, no one thought to write in a provision against tearing down your whole house—they didn't conceive that someone would want to do that."

"But if you want to replace your windows, then they want to know about that," Eric adds.

"You can replace like with like, but when we wanted to change a fixed window to a slider, we had to get permission," Linda recalls. "But we like the design review committee—we wish they were stricter."

FLAT-ROOF MODERN, 1954
Dallas, Texas
2,100 square feet
3 bedrooms, 2 baths

MINIMALIST
MASTERPIECE

Appearing almost institutional from the street, once you enter the hidden front door this house opens up and draws you in.

NO SOLICITING

◄ OVERLEAF: The same three colors used at the front door are seen on the outdoor panels (page 175), and the accent wall in the living room draws you in like a tractor beam. The brick load-bearing walls and gleaming ceramic tile entry floor are original, as are the windows, doors, and floating shelves throughout the home. A sculptural floor lamp, a mobile from fred flare, and a wooden dinosaur skeleton tell you that the inhabitants are modernists but not stuffy about it.

▶ THE LIVING ROOM FURNISHINGS are spare without being stark, but everything has its place. Extra seating cushions live under the long Nelson bench until put to use for parties, and a discontinued tri-level coffee table and the Eames lounge chair and ottoman are modern-made. The open red door leads to the master bedroom, and the area immediately behind the Noguchi Akari lamp is where floor-length curtains were designed to stack.

FIFTEEN YEARS AFTER BUYING THEIR CLEAN-LINED MODERN RANCH, DONNA AND CLIFF WELCH'S HOME is still turning heads. It's one of those overachievers, racking up awards from Preservation Dallas and the American Institute of Architects, and being featured on home tours, television, and in publications. Designed by Dallas architect Glenn Galaway for a structural engineer and his artist wife, it's in an out-of-the-way neighborhood near White Rock Lake. By now, with any earlier kinks and muddling remedied by the Welches, it's hitting its prime.

Like other homes of this era, the most striking features are hidden behind a purposefully quiet street presence. Floor-to-ceiling windows and a carport break up two 60'-long redbrick structures, one a low wall and the other the front facade. What looks like a simple rectangle from the front is in reality two interlocked L-shaped volumes with interesting ins and outs on the rear exterior.

"This is a basic house—it's not about beautiful wood or stone or a high-end kitchen or bath," says Cliff, owner of Welch Architecture in Dallas. "The materials in our home aren't really expensive, but the quality of construction is high. From the mason to the tile setter to the carpenter, they were all second- and third-generation craftsmen."

In the living room, three tall translucent fixed panes emit a soft light, while the clear upper sections open for ventilation. "Though the house has single-pane windows, it adapts well to the climate, with large overhangs on the south and west," Cliff mentions. "When it was built, it was tucked into probably 50-year-old trees, some of which we've since lost. Now it gets more sun than was ever intended."

A brilliant blue living room wall that repeats one of the outdoor colors focuses your attention on a minimal furniture arrangement, which they've had in various conformations for going on 10 years. A Nelson bench has served as a coffee table, but now is extra seating under a canvas by Cliff, while the modern couch previously faced the two Aalto armchairs. Where a sisal area rug grounded the grouping in years past, today the refinished oak floors are bare.

▸ **BENTWOOD AALTO CHAIRS** share a manufacturing methodology with the Eames leg splint on the wall near the bookshelves, and plywood is a recurring material elsewhere in the Welches' home. The UF4-J1 Akari light is a classic first manufactured in the 1950s, but the couple also has an inexpensive paper lantern hanging in their screened porch. Although there are bold uses of color, the neutral wood and tile floors and the black chairs ground everything.

"It takes us a long time to find what we really like," comments Donna, who formerly worked in the mortgage industry. "We're looking for area rugs for the living room and the family room. You walk in and there's the brick wall, and the blue wall, and the windows, and built-in cabinetry; those are all bold, so we need something basic that doesn't make a big statement."

Cliff differentiates between "expected" '50s furniture and their own choices, in part because some designs date back to the 1920s, such as the Wassily chair in the family room, while others are of more recent vintage, like the 1979 Diesis sofa by Antonio Citterio. "The architecture of the house is more timeless—it's about good modernism, not the '50s per se," he explains. "We have a mix of pieces you buy when you're first married and figure you'll retire when they wear out—like the headboard in our bedroom—or made from inexpensive materials—2x4s and slab doors, like our bed—and things that cost what some people pay for a car, such as the B&B Italia couch."

The idea of simple, honest materials handled with finesse is born out by the birch millwork and slab doors, the common brick, the plaster walls in the wet rooms, the gypsum board everywhere else, and the hardwood and natural cork floors. "The use of inexpensive materials is brought to another level through the detailing, which was carefully thought through," Cliff points out. "One example is the single profile of lumber used throughout the house that forms all of the doorframes, windowsills, jambs, mullions, transoms, floor base, and the transitions between dissimilar materials."

When he's not sounding like an architect, Cliff reveals he procrastinates almost as much as the next guy. The living room accent wall was baby blue when the Welches bought the house from Galaway's daughter, and for years they lived with trial color swatches while they deliberated the perfect hue. Just before a garage sale, when he figured they'd be showing curious neighbors the inside, Cliff begged for an hour to fix it and dumped samples of blue and yellow paint together for a mossy green that was up for several years. The yellow-orange painting over the Nelson bench was also done at the 11th hour before a home tour. Donna requested something with an Asian feel, and he whipped out the acrylic abstract and hung it, paint still wet, just before the first group came through.

The Welches, both 48, thought they'd change the color of that accent wall from time to time; as they added furnishings, the green worked less well. The other hues we see in the house—the brownish red and mustard on interior doors, the greens and taupes in the bedrooms and baths—replaced pastel midcentury shades.

"When we bought it, the exterior trim was gray, as were the decorative panels, but we found that the cemesto panels were originally daisy yellow and turquoise. I didn't think those original colors worked with the brick," Cliff says. "We shifted to earthier blues and yellows that didn't fight the landscape, but kept paint chip samples for future owners, just in case they might be full-bore purists."

▶ **THE SIDE AND REAR EXTERIOR WALLS** have Mondrian-inspired yellow, blue, and white panels. Recurring architectural elements include the low brick wall and the size and shape of the fenestration: the windows of the screen porch (near the chairs on the patio) are the same pattern as those on the right facade. The Welches have replaced high-maintenance plantings with grasses and gravel over a period of years.

"The use of inexpensive materials is brought to another level through the detailing, which was carefully thought through."

EDITED VIEWS

IF YOU HAVE BIG WALLS OF WINDOWS and a modernist home like the Welches' or the Eichler in the chapter "On Tract," it can seem like a shame to hang something in front of all that glass. If you don't mind being on display in your public rooms, and your climate is temperate, leaving them unadorned is the easiest and cleanest-looking solution.

"Window coverings are a tough one," says architect Cliff Welch. "In new construction, you can incorporate pockets in the ceiling for roller shades. We've used pleated shades in our bedrooms and baths, but it depends on the type of midcentury architecture. In some homes, venetian blinds work; this house was designed for curtains—there are natural places for the stacked curtains to nest." (See page 170.)

The roller shades Cliff mentions come in myriad neutrals, weaves, and in varying degrees of opacity, including solar shades that can reduce heat gain and block UV rays. IKEA, many online sites, and big-box stores carry these products. Out-of-the-way installations, such as high clerestory windows, can be operated by remote control.

The opaque glass in the Welches' home was often used in bathrooms of all types of ranches, allowing sunlight in but not direct views. You can achieve that same effect with window film, a solution employed at the San Mateo Eichler prior to the installation of the privacy fence. Searching online for "window film" will generate lots of choices, from rice paper–like patterns to geometrics and frosted glass looks.

There is also much to be said for curtains: they're classically period correct and provide a measure of protection from both heat gain and winter condensation. They work in both traditional and modern ranches—the diverse homes in the chapters "Full Metal Jacket," "Retro Gem," and "Artists' Collective" all have floor-length curtains—and offer another chance to express your personal style. Avoid tab-top drapes and the opulent floor-puddling style, and research mounting options early on. The most successful installations are cable systems or minimal tracks that fade into the room's natural datum lines, as opposed to finial curtain rods mounted on the wall above the windows as in more traditional homes. Sites like The Shade Store, Smith+Noble, and West Elm are a good way to educate yourself about both hardware and coverings.

If you're not allergic to the '70s, mini blinds are still an option and, in a late-'40s to mid-'50s standard ranch, metal venetian blinds, alone or in concert with tie-back vintage-look curtains, can be spot-on. Even such mainstream choices as cellular and Silhouette-type shades can look clean and modern if they're inside-mounted.

In homes of this era, please—no fancy valances, wooden shutters, or poufy Roman shades. And unless you want to make a statement like Jennie Hall does with her bold barkcloth drapes (see the chapter "Retro Gem"), window dressing should be a background player that allows your architecture and furnishings to shine.

Solar shades, like these paisley ones from The Shade Store, fit inside the window frame and virtually disappear when they're rolled up.

Venetian blinds—or mini blinds if you're on a budget—and pinch-pleat draperies paired with plain wood valances is a great look for the living room of this early '40s ranch.

"The materials in our home aren't really expensive, but the quality of construction is high."

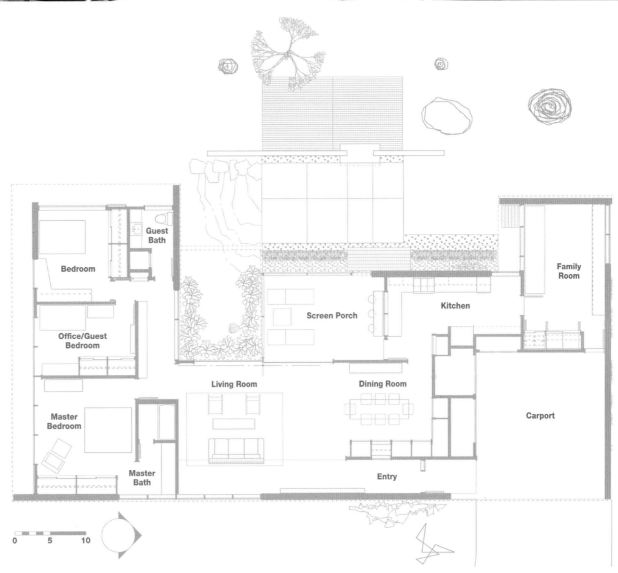

Guest Bath

Bedroom

Office/Guest Bedroom

Master Bedroom

Master Bath

Screen Porch

Living Room

Kitchen

Dining Room

Family Room

Carport

Entry

0   5   10

Through the red door off the living room is the master bedroom, and down a glass-walled hall with a built-in bookcase are son Dylan's room and a third bedroom used as an office. Cliff built their two plat-form beds some years ago, and other furnishings are kept to a minimum, particularly in the master bedroom. There, a series of matted black-and-white photos pick up the white of the bedspread and the B&B Italia dresser, which has contrasting blue and orange drawers that reference the grid of the exte-rior panels. Everything else is built in and put away.

"People ask how we can live with a minimum of clutter," Cliff comments. "It's the built-in storage: in the carport there's room for everything that usually takes up space in a garage, and in the dining area there are places for coats, Christmas decorations, wine storage, stereo gear—that's what makes it possible."

▲ **LOOKING TOWARD** the en suite bath, the closet doors are MDF, and the vanity has a white Carrara marble top. The crisp, stacked trim seen at the windows, closet, and whenever materials change—from plaster to mirror to brown plaster over the vanity, for instance—emphasizes the home's organizing principles. A Hubbell Vaportite light fixture adds some industrial panache by the windows.

▶ **THE ORIGINAL INTERIOR DOORS** are painted in a palette of blue, black, yellow, or red, here in con-trast to the neutral taupe of the master bedroom. Ceilings in the house are 9' tall, with a datum line at 7' that incorporates light-sharing glazing. The bed frame is made out of two solid-core doors, and the discontinued dresser is from B&B Italia; Design Within Reach offers a similar look in their Brix storage line.

The **plywood headboard and storage units** tie in thematically to the living room furnishings and vintage Eames splint.

◄ IN DYLAN'S ROOM, Cliff Welch made the Baltic birch plywood headboard and designed the storage units, which were custom-built and incorporate repurposed Blu Dot doors. The Eames Aluminum Group chair is vintage, and the entry and storage doors are painted the same bold yellow. At the windows are fitted pleated shades and, at desk-level, ribbed opaque glass.

▲ OFF CAMERA, a new Kohler toilet replaced the original in the hallway bath when it stopped working, and maple plywood and Häfele pulls dress up the marble-topped vanity. Tolomeo wall sconces augment the natural light, and original floating shelves held up by angle irons embedded in the brick wall offer display areas here as well as in the entry hall and dining room.

The vanity in the hall bath near Dylan's room was painted plywood, so Cliff replaced that material with maple veneer, but the sink, counter, brick wall, and shower tile are original. If the house had changed hands more, the brick would likely be painted or faced with another material by now, a practice Cliff isn't dead set against, necessarily.

"It depends on the brick: if they are clean modules that have held up well like our Acme ferrous red commons, it would be a sin," he says. "On the other hand, if the brick is rough or the original color palette is hard to work with, you might want to paint it; Alvar Aalto has some painted brick that is wonderful. But approach that decision cautiously and know it's irreversible."

▲▶ **DOUBLING BACK FROM THE BEDROOM WING,** you can go through the wide sliding glass doors to the screened porch, or past the B&B Italia couch into the dining area, which has an intimate quality and loads of storage. Cliff made the seven-plus-foot table from a maple slab door and an office supply store base, and they found the 1920s-designed Marcel Breuer chairs at a garage sale.

Although the dining room has no windows, the warmth of the glazed birch cabinetry and the proximity to the living room's openness makes that a nice change of pace.

Like other homeowners, the Welches advise against wholesale changes the second you move in, though they did a few early whirlwind projects themselves.

"I immediately thought the finish on the birch cabinets in the dining room was dated," Cliff remembers. "I took one door off and sanded it, thinking a natural finish would be better. But as we lived there and considered the options, I realized that the original fruitwood glaze gave it depth and we came to appreciate it."

Around the corner from the dining room, the kitchen is a melding of vintage and stylistically appropriate new materials. "It had been the hub of the house, with cooking, laundry, and ironing all in one room," Donna says. "Things were very tight and there was maybe three feet of space down the center."

The '50s Hotpoint metal cabinets needed resurfacing, so the couple sanded and prepped the cabinets for the painter, who sprayed them with two-part auto enamel in a booth in their carport. White vinyl tile and a rotted subfloor were replaced with 12" natural cork squares with an inlaid decorative motif. And by borrowing a little space from the carport, they were able to recess the refrigerator into the wall and add narrow storage where the washer and dryer once were.

◄ REFINISHED METAL CABINETS turn the whole kitchen into a magnet-friendly gallery, with one of Dylan's drawings on display in this view. Instead of the original daisy yellow Formica counters, the couple chose dark laminate with a wood edge; it's twice as thick as usual, with a $1/8$" aluminum insert that speaks to the stainless steel backsplash by the sink. The Welches installed a new Viking dishwasher and under-counter GE Monogram refrigerator, but the '50s Hotpoint oven is still in place. Note the decorative inset in the new cork floors, and that the windows over the sink form a pass-through to the screened porch (see page 187).

▲ OPPOSITE THE OVEN, the Frigidaire refrigerator has been recessed into the wall and wrapped with an L-shaped orange furrdown that conceals the HVAC ducting. This accent color is also seen in the living room, the bath, and the family media room. With the laundry hookups moved to a hall closet, there's room for a narrow birch cabinet with blue and metallic accents.

▼ **IN THE REVERSE VIEW,** we see a modest nook with stools for a quick coffee break next to the doorway leading to the family room. The Viking range top, while thoroughly modern, has a more utilitarian look when teamed with the brick backsplash and laminate counter, and Cliff's choice of a black flat storage file across from it furthers that notion. The cooling rack to the left of the stove solves the problem of where to set hot pots, and the dark counter and toe-kick area repeat the black accents in the living/dining room.

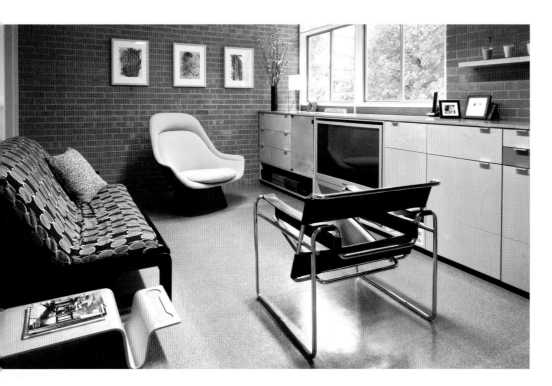

Off the kitchen, the cork floor continues into the former art workshop, now a kid-friendly family room with built-in cabinets for media, games, and the like. A futon, reupholstered vintage lounge chair, and the Wassily chair fill the narrow space.

Although their son is now middle-school age, even when he was young he was expected to enjoy and adapt to his environment, not vice versa. "People warned us modern houses with lots of glass are not good for a baby," Donna recalls. "But the windows and wildlife made Dylan more connected to the world. We didn't feel the need to put bumpers on every corner or change our furniture; if kids bump into the glass, they do it once, not twice."

The minimalism is carried outside to the landscaping, too. A screened porch is in use most of the year, as is a deck and a patio that the Welches added. But there is continual maintenance involved in keeping this aging beauty looking her best.

▲ THE WELCHES

worked with the tight dimensions of the former studio by building wall-spanning storage for electronics, floor pillows, and the television set. A practical futon and bent plywood side table are paired with a high-back '60s Warren Platner lounge chair and the chrome and black leather Wassily chair.

The large screened windows and sliding glass doors virtually erase the distinction between inside and out.

▲ THE SCREENED PORCH AND OUTDOORS are furnished with Skate lounges, side tables, and armchairs by Paul Tuttle, the same functional Grainger shop stools as in the kitchen, and modern butterfly chairs and Knoll Toledo chairs paired with an Overstock.com dining table on the patio. The floor is ebony stained concrete.

▶ **THE GRID THEME**
is continued in the walls of
the screened porch, which
makes it read as inherent to
the architecture and not an
afterthought. Working with
Hocker Design Group, the
Welches added the cattle
trough water feature and the
floating concrete patio, which
steps down to a cantilevered
deck (see page 175), making
the transition from inside to
outside progressively elegant.

"An older house is a lot of work: there's condensation on the windows during the winter, and
old houses move—cracks and peeling paint are
things you have to contend with," Cliff says. "We
may move someday, but I don't think we could go
back to a two-story home; we wouldn't feel so
connected. People say you lose the front porch
with a ranch, but we find that in this type of neighborhood, friends know to walk to the back to drop
in—that's where we'll be."

"Though the house has single-pane windows, it adapts well to the climate, with large overhangs on the south and west. Now it gets more sun than was ever intended."

CREDITS

Work of Art: Floor plan, Mark Engberg, COLAB Architecture + Urban Design; Suburban Modern brochure, Sherwin-Williams

Family Matters: Floor plan, Nancy Anderson, Arroyo Design

Full Metal Jacket: Floor plan and Care-free Home brochure images courtesy Alcoa Inc.; Kerf cabinets © 2008 Julia Kuskin

Retro Gem: Floor plan, Nancy Anderson, Arroyo Design; vintage black-and-white images, Jack Moncrief Photography, courtesy his heirs; Atomic Doodle wallpaper © Bradbury & Bradbury Art Wallpapers; op art wallpaper, Rosie's Vintage Wallpaper; Northstar appliances © Elmira Stove Works

Crank Up the Volume: Floor plans, Pam Kinzie, Kinzie & Associates; San Raphael toilet and Vox Vessel sink © Kohler Co., used by permission; Appiani tile © Nemo Tile

On Tract: Site plan, Mark Marcinik, M110 Architecture

Artists' Collective: Floor plans, Nancy Anderson, Arroyo Design

Minimalist Masterpiece: Site plan, Clifford Welch, Welch Architecture; solar shades © the Shade Store

RESOURCES

ACCESSORIES & MISCELLANEOUS

3form: www.3-form.com
Bose: www.bose.com
Cincinnati Form Follows Function: www.cf3.org
Cincinnati Modern: www.cincinnatimodern.com
Denyse Schmidt Quilts: www.dsquilts.com/quilts.asp
Hip Haven: www.hiphaven.com
Howard Miller Clock Company: www.howardmiller.com
Retro Renovation: www.retrorenovation.com
The Shade Store: www.theshadestore.com
Smith+Noble: www.smithandnoble.com

ART

Mequitta Ahuja: www.automythography.com
Boris Bally: www.borisbally.com
Christian Carlson: www.christiancarlson.net
Katharine Cobey: www.katharinecobey.com
Anthony Corradetti Glassblowing Studio: www.corradetti.com
Laurie Danial: www.lauriedanial.com
Toni Doilney: www.tonidoilney.com

Joshua Hagler: www.joshuahagler.com
Charley Harper: www.charleyharperartstudio.com
Linda Hesh: www.lindahesh.com
Laurel Lukaszewski: www.laurellukaszewski.com
Robert Ernst Marx: www.roberternstmarx.com
Chris Newhard: www.baywoodartists.com/Chris_Newhard_Bio.html
Mick Park: www.artsetter.com/member/mick-park
Stashu Smaka: www.stashusmaka.com
Alexandra Solmssen: www.alexsolmssen.com
Dan Steinhilber: www.artnet.com/artists/dan%2Dsteinhilber
David Thai: www.davidthai.ca
Taman VanScoy: www.tamanvanscoy.com

DESIGN

Artisan Metalwork, Stashu Smaka:
Portland, Oregon, www.artisanmetalwork.com

Big Branch Woodworking, Neel Briggs:
Portland, Oregon, www.bigbranchwoodworking.com

COLAB Architecture + Urban Design, Mark Engberg:
Portland, Oregon, www.colabarchitecture.com

Custom Metal Fab:
Scappoose, Oregon, www.cmfstainless.com

Glenn Pope Woodworking:
Calistoga, California, 707-942-5393

Hocker Design Group:
Dallas, Texas, www.hockerdesign.com

Kinzie & Associates, Pam Kinzie:
Calistoga, California, 707-942-8357

M110 Architecture, Mark Marcinik:
San Francisco, California, 415-334-7670

Modernpast, Ric Lopez:
San Francisco, California, www.modernpast.com

NWR Construction, Ron Downey:
Portland, Oregon, 503-231-9444

Organic Matters, Tom Peloquin:
Portland, Oregon, 503-320-2458

Welch Architecture, Clifford Welch:
Dallas, Texas, www.welcharchitecture.com

Windsmith Design, Mark Bourne:
San Carlos, California, www.windsmithdesign.com

FLOOR & WALL COVERINGS
Armstrong: www.armstrong.com
Azrock: www.azrock.com
Bradbury & Bradbury Art Wallpapers: www.bradbury.com
California Paints: www.californiapaints.com
Eco-Friendly Flooring: www.ecofriendlyflooring.com
FLOR: www.myflor.com
Forbo Flooring Systems (Marmoleum): www.forboflooringna.com
Kaleen: www.kaleen.com
Milliken Floor Covering: www.millikencarpet.com
Odegard: www.odegardinc.com/flash/index.html
Rosie's Vintage Wallpaper: www.rosiesvintagewallpaper.com
Secondhand Rose: www.secondhandrose.com
Sherwin-Williams: www.sherwin-williams.com

FURNITURE
Altura Furniture: www.alturafurniture.com
B&B Italia: www.bandbitalia.com
Blu Dot: www.bludot.com
Bolier & Company: www.bolierco.com
CB2: www.cb2.com
Cherner Chair Company: www.chernerchair.com
Crate & Barrel: www.crateandbarrel.com
Dellarobbia: www.dellarobbiausa.com
Design Within Reach: www.dwr.com
Ekornes: www.ekornes.com/us
Fritz Hansen: www.fritzhansen.com
Grainger: www.grainger.com
Herman Miller: www.hermanmiller.com
Knoll: www.knoll.com
Living Divani: www.livingdivani.it
Marcel Wanders: www.marcelwanders.com
Modernica: www.modernica.net
Scandinavian Designs: www.scandinaviandesigns.com
Techline USA: www.techlineusa.com
West Elm: www.westelm.com
Williams-Sonoma: www.williams-sonoma.com

HARDWARE & FIXTURES
American Standard: www.americanstandard-us.com
Blomus: www.blomus.com

Dornbracht: www.dornbracht.com
Duravit: www.duravit.com
Fry Reglet: www.fryreglet.com
Grohe: www.groheamerica.com
Häfele: www.hafele.com
Hansgrohe: www.hansgrohe-usa.com
Hoesch: www.hoesch.de
Kohler: www.kohler.com
Majestic: www.majesticproducts.com
Modern Fan Co.: www.modernfan.com
Neo-Metro: www.neo-metro.com
Oliveri: www.oliverisinks.com
Toto: www.totousa.com
Valli&Valli: www.vallivalli-us.com
Vola: www.vola.com
Zuma Collection: www.zumacollection.com

KITCHEN & BATH
Amana: www.amana.com
Asko Appliances: www.askousa.com
Baci Mirrors: www.bacimirrors.com
Bella Tile Co.: www.bellatilenyc.com
Bertazzoni: www.bertazzoni.com
Big Chill: www.bigchill.com
Bosch: www.bosch-home.com
Daltile: www.daltile.com
DuPont Corian: www.dupont.com
Electrolux: www.electrolux.com
Elmira Stove Works: www.elmirastoveworks.com
Florida Tile: www.floridatile.com
Formica: www.formica.com
Frigidaire: www.frigidaire.com
Gaggenau: www.gaggenau.com
General Electric: www.geappliances.com
Henrybuilt: www.henrybuilt.com
IKEA: www.ikea.com
James Hardie: www.jameshardie.com
Jenn-Air: www.jennair.com
Kerf Design: www.kerfdesign.com
Nemo Tile: www.nemotile.com

Pratt & Larson Ceramics: www.prattandlarson.com
Restoration Hardware: www.restorationhardware.com
Thermador: www.thermador.com
Viking Range: www.vikingrange.com
Westinghouse: www.westinghouse.com
Wilsonart: www.wilsonart.com
Wolf Appliance: www.wolfappliance.com

LIGHTING

Akari light sculptures: http://akaristore.stores.yahoo.net/akari.html
Flos: www.flos.com
Hampstead Lighting: www.hampsteadlighting.com
Hubbell: www.hubbelloutdoor.com
LBL Lighting: www.lbllighting.com
Moon Shine Lamp and Shade: www.moonshineshades.com
Pablo: www.pablodesigns.com
Remcraft Lighting Products: www.remcraft.com/ar
Tango: www.tangolighting.com

MIDCENTURY DESIGN ICONS

Alvar Aalto: www.aalto.com
Arapahoe Acres: www.arapahoeacres.org
Harry Bertoia: www.harrybertoia.org
Marcel Breuer: www.marcelbreuer.org
Alexander Calder: www.calder.org
Charles and Ray Eames: www.eamesoffice.com/charles-and-ray
Joseph Eichler: www.eichlernetwork.com/article/joe-eichler-profile
Eichler X-100 house: www.eichlernetwork.com/article/eichler-x-100-house-steel
Vladimir Kagan: www.vladimirkagancouture.com
Le Corbusier: www.cassinausa.com/corbusier.html
Paul McCobb: www.architonic.com/dcobj/paul-mccobb/8101346/2/1
Ludwig Mies van der Rohe: www.designboom.com/portrait/mies/bg.html
George Nelson: www.georgenelson.org
Isamu Noguchi: www.noguchi.org
Adrian Pearsall: www.adrianpearsall.com
Warren Platner: www.dwr.com/category/designers/m-p/warren-platner.do
Eero Saarinen: http://scandinaviandesign.com/Eero_saarinen/index.htm
Russel Wright: www.russelwrightstudios.com

WINDOWS & DOORS

Arcadia: www.arcadiaincorporated.com
Blomberg Window Systems: www.blombergwindowsystems.com
Marlin Windows: www.marlinwindows.com
Milgard: www.milgard.com
Peerless Products: www.peerlessproducts.com
Pickens Window Parts: www.pickenswindowparts.com
Simpson Door Company: www.simpsondoor.com
Tafco Corporation: www.tafcocorp.com
Wayne-Dalton: www.wayne-dalton.com/index.html

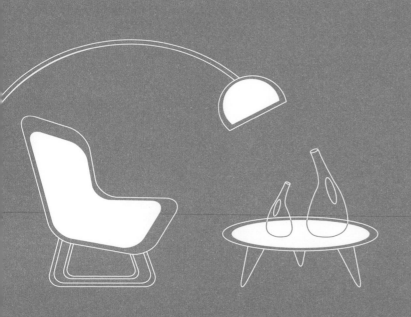